FISH OUT OF WATER
HAS SOMETHING FOR EVERYONE

I wish this book had been available when I was teaching 6th grade in public schools, serving congregations, working with youth groups, teaching seminarians, and working with ecumenical and intercultural groups. This book names the structural power dynamics and differences between and among us, offering both analyses and ways to work toward mutual cultural competence. I particularly appreciate the threads connecting individual stories from one chapter to the next, the variety of examples, and the direct questions for readers' reflection. I commend *Fish Out of Water* to all of us who work with individuals and groups; it is wise, challenging counsel.

—**The Rev. Dr. Susan E. Davies,**
Professor and Dean
Bangor Theological Seminary

Fish Out of Water is an excellent resource for exploring the many ways that people feel marginalized, voiceless, and powerless at school, in the workplace, and in society in general. The real value of this book lies in the courageous conversations it will certainly provoke among those fish who swim in the middle of the pond [and] work to create more inclusive environments where others can be seen, heard, acknowledged, and helped to THRIVE.

—**Stephanie Graham-Rivas,** Retired
Los Angeles County Office of Education
Author of *Culturally Proficient Inquiry* and
Culturally Proficient Leadership for Equity

Fish Out of Water weaves interdisciplinary concepts with piercing case studies and self-assessment exercises. Readers will engage in a process of critical reflection related to the real life experience of not fitting in. This comprehensive treatment integrates grounded theory with multiple realities. It is a must-read for leaders.

—**John Robert Browne**
Author of *Walking the Equity Talk: A Guide for Culturally Courageous Leadership in School Communities*

A Fish Out of Water is just as valuable as all other fish. This book is an invaluable resource for leading change in an organization, beginning with the most critical resource in the organization, professional capital, the people.

—**Diann Kitamura**, Associate Superintendent
Santa Rosa City Schools

This book made me think, reflect, consider, and reconsider my position as an educator of young children. They deserve to know we care enough to share the codes they need in order to thrive in our human pond and the rest of the ponds they will encounter throughout their lives. Seeing, caring, and sharing codes will facilitate the eventual co-creation of the third mutually shared set of cultural expectations.

—**Renee Bundy**, Director
Sequoia Nursery School

Fish Out of Water provides a creative, nonthreatening way to address one of the most difficult issues confronting schools, the workforce and daily living—learning cultural codes to survive in today's culturally diverse society. This book offers a simple yet never simplistic opportunity to examine and reflect on one's cultural proficiency. In an engaging and witty manner this book provides a coherent set of principles for swimming regardless of the body of water.

—**Raymond W. Jones**, Professor, Neurocognitive Trainer, and Co-Founder of PranaMind

Fish Out of Water sheds much needed light on issues of diversity, inclusion, and identity. It is refreshing to see critical societal issues through the lens of individual experience and organizational cultures. What an important contribution and accessible educational tool for all institutions interested in doing the good work of cultural competency.

—Nehanda Imara
Merritt College African American Studies

Fish Out of Water is well written, informative, and thought provoking, providing powerful insight into how we navigate our personal and professional lives. For many people, code switching is a determinant of professional success or psychological survival; it is a discussion that needs to be on the table. A great read, valuable information.

—Jason Wall, Associate Director
Career Center, University of California Irvine

This book was amazing—thank you for taking the time and emotional energy to put it together. It will help many people; I could just see myself and many of my LGBT sisters and brothers throughout the pages. I only wish this book had been available to my parents, clergy, and teachers when I was a child Fish Out of Water and then to me as I grew into a young adult Fish Out of Water. The warmth of the stories, the scholarly description of our social structure, and the clarity of strategies made this a standout read for me.

—The Rev. Dr. Georgia Prescott, Chair
Diversity Commission,
Centers for Spiritual Living

This book made me think. It is a courageous attempt at the difficult subject of who "doesn't fit" into the spaces and places we inhabit—and why. But the most valuable part of this book is that it describes what we can do about making our schools, workplaces, and communities more inclusive, and ultimately more effective.

—Nicki King, PhD
Reducing Mental Health Disparities Project,
University of California Davis

Fish Out of Water is a testament to the courage of every person who has ever felt different. In this global community, cultural competency and code switching are required skills for success in any relationship and any environment. For those who want to better understand others while transforming themselves into the best they can be, *Fish Out of Water* is a must-read!

—Tadia Rice
Author and Education Consultant

Nuri-Robins and Bundy brilliantly explain a phenomenon I am sure I share with others. Their stories illustrate the myriad ways we Fish Out of Water experience life and shed light on how we can overcome it. Longing for belonging, finding a place that fits can be a challenge, but Nuri-Robins and Bundy have found a way to help those of us not so deft at the human experience. Their insight is profound and necessary.

—Arrowyn Ambrose,
Founder and Creative Director,
Story Tribe

Fish Out of Water is both a practical guide for those who find themselves or someone they care about in the wrong pond and a promising road map for navigating the often confusing and painful path of those who don't fit in. Readers will benefit from the language the authors have created so that parents, teachers, mentors, supervisors, and coaches can be helpful resources to the Fish Out of Water in their lives.

—Sally Vasen Alter
Leadership Consultant and Executive Coach

Expect the unexpected in *Fish Out of Water*, where you will learn through compelling true stories what it means to be out of place in an academic, social, or corporate environment. If you are seeking help for yourself or for the people you teach, supervise, mentor, or care about, you will gain insight through questions for reflections and guidelines for book study. You will be able to recognize and successfully guide your fish out of water to discover their personal power.

—**Flora Morris Brown, PhD,**
Publishing Coach and Author of
Color Your Life Happy: Create Your
Unique Path and Claim the Joy You Deserve

The need for this book cannot be overstated. Each of us has been a Fish Out of Water in one setting or another, and many of us have been so in many settings. This book helps not only those of us who identify with the Fish Out of Water, but also those of us who are in positions to help others who may need help to swim comfortably in their ponds. This user-friendly format readily enables readers to help Fish Out of Water to develop strategies for swimming comfortably through the pond, ensure that the Fish Out of Water have safe places to swim, or, sometimes, aid them to find a safe channel for swimming to a different, more suitable pond.

—**Shari Dorantes Hatch**
Writer and Editor

As someone who has rarely fit well into a group or social situation, the brilliant concepts and practical code-switching skills revealed in this book have explained to me what I thought was inexplicable. Nuri-Robins and Bundy offer ways to decode human interactions along with methods for a framework to thrive instead of flounder! This book is a survival guide for any creative person.

—**Diana Folsom**, Head of Collections Digitization
Gilcrease Museum, Tulsa, OK

A worthwhile read for anyone who wants to be a better (and more empathetic) boss, colleague, parent, and friend. As I read the stories woven through the book, I reflected on my personal experiences with every Fish Out of Water I've ever known and came to terms with the one profound, life-changing experience I had as a misfit which almost derailed my career. Aha! moments abound.

—**Paula Van Ness**, President and CEO
Connecticut Community Foundation

This book is of immense value because it explains what it means to live as a Fish Out of Water. The wisdom, guidance, and support will help you to navigate the rivers of your life.

—**K. Rashid Nuri**, Founder and CEO
Truly Living Well Center for
Natural Urban Agriculture

There's no expiration date on learning, and *Fish Out of Water* is definitive proof. This book is a crucial component in navigating your way through social and work relationships.

—**Gail Mitchell**, Senior Correspondent
Billboard Magazine

Fish Out of Water

To Ray and Randy
To the Memory of Andre Cunningham

Fish Out of Water

Mentoring, Managing, and Self-Monitoring People Who Don't Fit In

Kikanza Nuri-Robins
Lewis Bundy

CORWIN

A SAGE Publishing Company

FOR INFORMATION:

Corwin

A SAGE Company

2455 Teller Road

Thousand Oaks, California 91320

(800) 233-9936

www.corwin.com

SAGE Publications Ltd.

1 Oliver's Yard

55 City Road

London, EC1Y 1SP

United Kingdom

SAGE Publications India Pvt. Ltd.

B 1/I 1 Mohan Cooperative Industrial Area

Mathura Road, New Delhi 110 044

India

SAGE Publications Asia-Pacific Pte. Ltd.

3 Church Street

#10-04 Samsung Hub

Singapore 049483

Program Director: Dan Alpert

Senior Associate Editor: Kimberly Greenberg

Editorial Assistant: Katie Crilley

Production Editor: Amy Schroller

Copy Editor: Karin Rathert

Typesetter: C&M Digitals (P) Ltd.

Proofreader: Sally Jaskold

Indexer: David Luljak

Cover Designer: Scott Van Atta

Marketing Manager: Charline Maher

Printed in the United States of America

Library of Congress Cataloging-in-Publication Data

Names: Nuri-Robins, Kikanza, 1950- author. | Bundy, Lewis, author.

Title: Fish out of water : mentoring, managing, and self-monitoring people who don't fit in / Kikanza Nuri-Robins, Lewis Bundy.

Description: Thousand Oaks, California : Corwin, a SAGE Company, [2016] | Includes bibliographical references and index.

Identifiers: LCCN 2015045197 | ISBN 978-1-5063-0302-4 (pbk. : acid-free paper)

Subjects: LCSH: Cultural competence. | Intercultural communication. | Marginality, Social. | Social perception. | Cultural pluralism. | Multiculturalism.

Classification: LCC HM793.R63 2016 | DDC 303.48/2—dc23

LC record available at http://lccn.loc.gov/2015045197

This book is printed on acid-free paper.

16 17 18 19 20 10 9 8 7 6 5 4 3 2 1

Contents

We Wear the Mask

We wear the mask that grins and lies,
It hides our cheeks and shades our eyes,—
This debt we pay to human guile;
With torn and bleeding hearts we smile,
And mouth with myriad subtleties.

Why should the world be over-wise,
In counting all our tears and sighs?
Nay, let them only see us, while
We wear the mask.

We smile, but, O great Christ, our cries
To thee from tortured souls arise.
We sing, but oh the clay is vile
Beneath our feet, and long the mile;
But let the world dream otherwise,
We wear the mask!

Paul Laurence Dunbar (*Lyrics of Lowly Life,*
Dodd Mead & Co., 1896, p. 167)

Foreword

Terry Cross introduced the Cultural Proficiency framework in his seminal monograph, "Towards a Culturally Competent System of Care" (1989).

Thirty years ago when I first developed the Cultural Competence Continuum as an overhead illustration for a lecture in the first of many Cultural Competence classes I would teach, I had no idea what an influential and long-lasting concept it would become. I recall that my first iteration began at Cultural Destruction and ended at Competence. I proudly showed it to one of my mentors at the time, because I wanted to know what he thought of it. He looked at it for some time without saying anything, and when I probed for a reaction he said, "Well, this is disappointing." As he looked up at me, he must have caught my crestfallen look, because he then said, "No, it's not that. I mean, shouldn't we be striving for more than just Competence?"

I realized he was right, and while I had advocated for human service providers and organizations to develop basic Cultural Competence, it was not enough. Advanced Competence or Cultural Proficiency was the ultimate goal. Where the Culturally Competent provider or agency functions effectively in the context of cultural differences, the Culturally Proficient professional or agency uses the power of culture to heal, teach, help, or serve.

I have been pleased with and admire Kikanza and Lewis' focus on the Proficiency end of the Continuum. They and others like them are stretching what we know about cross-cultural practice, both in the sense of what it is possible for individuals to do and what organizations can do. Their insights into code switching and their intentional approach to the development of related-life skills takes the theoretical and makes it practical. Their straightforward treatment of Cultural Proficiency and the clarity of the framework provide the reader with a solid foundation for learning and applying their approach. It is exciting to see a work that applies theory to real life and includes implications and strategies for both individuals and organizations.

The authors have built on the Cultural Competence Model in ways that I and my coauthors of the 1989 monograph can feel very satisfied about, but there is so much yet to be done. Still today, most uninformed organizations and individuals treat culture as if it is a problem to solve when, in reality, it is one of the greatest resources available to aid our work in human services. Cultural Proficiency harnesses the power of culture and applies it to the helping relationship. Knowing how culture functions in our lives and in the lives of those we seek to help gives one access to powerful tools for helping. In this new book the authors pursue one thread of this potential. They examine the marginal person, the Fish Out of Water.

I know this awkward place between cultures very well. I am a product of two different cultures and acculturated into a third. Raised by a White, hardworking farmer father and a generous and culturally wise Seneca mother, I found that I seldom fit in. The values, communication patterns, and cultural behaviors of my mother did not fit with the expectations of the mainstream school. My orientation to farm life and being a loner along with an unbridled curiosity made me the odd duck to cousins and peers alike. My adaption was to turn inward and to feel my difference as a deficit, with a resulting negative self-esteem, introverted behavior, and low school performance.

It was not until I found social work that my two cultures began to meld into what I could understand as complementary assets. This third culture, the professional culture of social work, would be the space that I could become myself. As an American Indian social worker, it was my discovery that my behavior and values were normal Indigenous ways of being in the world, passed on to me by my mother, that allowed me to begin to appreciate my culture and build a positive identity and a meaningful career. This realization was both freeing and fraught with challenges.

As a person of two cultures it was sometimes hard to be accepted easily in either one. Fortunately, I had kind and loving mentors who helped me. After graduate school I went back to my reservation to work. It was to be the best and the hardest time in my life. Racism was prevalent in the border town where I worked. My White education was not well accepted by my own people. My biracial heritage set me apart as a target for both sides.

One day as I sat with an elder who knew the situation, I lamented how difficult it was to not fit in. He asked me, "Do you know what makes a bridge strong?" I responded with something like steel or concrete. He said, "No, a bridge is only strong if it has a strong foundation on both sides. Your White man's education is your strong foundation on that side. Your mother's values and teachings are your foundation in our culture. You are a bridge. Your strength is to serve as a bridge between our people and the White world."

These words would forever change how I would feel about myself. They moved me from being a Fish Out of Water to becoming a valuable human being. This elder was a Culturally Proficient helper. He knew how to heal with words, stories, ceremonies, and songs. He was coach, teacher, advisor, and guide, but most of all, a Culturally Proficient, natural therapist. His knowledge of human nature was deep and wise and I learned more about myself from his quiet teaching and his gentle teasing than from any other mentor.

With the knowledge that this book brings, you too may be able to recognize and help the Fish Out of Water find their place. Given the world we live in, their gifts, talents, and insights are desperately needed. If anyone is to become Culturally Proficient in helping the next generations of our nation it will be the Fish Out of Water.

Terry Cross, Senior Advisor
National Indian Child Welfare Association
Portland, Oregon

Acknowledgments

Many people helped in the writing of this book.

Thanks to our many friends and colleagues who participated in interviews and focus groups. It is from them that we learned of the innumerable ways people code switch and ultimately share codes with those in their environment. They told us heart wrenching stories and stories of triumph. Thank you all for your contributions.

Thank you to the many friends and colleagues who gave us permission to use their stories in this book. The stories are true; the quotations reflect what people actually said, and the names have no relationship to the person quoted.

Many of our colleagues read iterations of the manuscript and provided praise, criticism, and redirection, all of which helped us to finish this project. Thank you.

Our editor, Dan Alpert, shepherded us through the process of writing the proposal and finding our voices as long-time friends and colleagues but new coauthors. We appreciate his faith in this work and constant encouragement through the process. Thanks, Dan.

And finally, a big thanks to Lewis for showing up, saying yes, and pushing me to swim into the deep areas of the pond.

Kikanza Nuri-Robins
Los Angeles, CA

I am grateful to the many people who provided motivation, encouragement, and insight for the completion of this work.

To my base group of Sherri, Amber, Savannah, Sierra, and Patrick, Ashley, Ayan and Onyx, because they have been the inspiration and the victims of my stories all of their lives.

To the family that shaped and shared my life, Dot's Lot; Mary, Lorece, Maurice, Diane (mom would be proud of all of us), Myla, Dee Dee, Dwayne, Billy, Lawrence, Derrick, Diedra, Tanisha, Adrian, and their children; and to Rabiah and Sonya . . . Bob and Dimple Santos . . . all of whom have had to bear the burden of my yarns at one time or another.

To my precious friends, whose support and love I will always treasure. Among them are Raymond and Aaliyah Jones; Nehanda and Nia Imara; Ardise Rawlins; Konstance and Gail Mitchell; Carnell, Sharon, Brian and Celisse Pinkney; Aunt Claudia and the Porterville Clan; Ravenswood High School Class of '67; the cantankerous members of The Brothers Golf Club, and my co-conspirator and motivator, Kikanza.

And especially, for putting up with me and all that comes with that, my wife, Ardise Renee.

Thank you all.

Lewis Bundy
Oakland, CA

PUBLISHER'S ACKNOWLEDGMENTS

Corwin gratefully acknowledges the contributions of the following reviewers:

Vera Blake
Educational Consultant
ASCD Faculty Member
Dumfries, VA

David G. Daniels
High School Principal
Susquehanna
   Valley Central Schools
Conklin, NY

Kathy Tritz-Rhodes
Principal
MMC Primary and
   MMC East Elementary
Cleghorn, IA

Bonnie Tyron, EdD
Mentor Coach & Retired
   Principal
Cobleskill-Richmondville
   Central School
Cobleskill, NY

Introduction

Everyone wants to belong to something or to someone. Everyone wants to have a place where people know who you are and want you there because of, not in spite of, who you are. This book is about learning to manage self and others when they don't belong to the groups they are in.

Fish Out of Water are people who have not learned to discern and respond appropriately to the cultural expectations—the cultural codes—of their environment and consequently are targeted and marginalized by members of the dominant group. This book is for three groups of people who seek to learn or teach the cultural expectations of an organization:

- People with a life pattern of not fitting in
- People who manage people who don't fit in
- Adults who work with kids who are targeted and bullied because they are different

We, Kikanza and Lewis, are Fish Out of Water who are accepted by and relatively comfortable in most ponds that are not of our choosing. We have learned the cultural codes of our environments and have learned to code switch effectively. We have spent our professional lives (approximately forty years each) helping people to decipher organizational cultures and to enhance their personal power by learning

1

to code switch. As organizational development consultants, much of our work is spent advocating for children who are Fish Out of Water and coaching adults who are Fish Out of Water or who manage them.

Most books in the diversity and inclusion genre address members of the dominant culture and provide information on how to change dysfunctional, oppressive, inequitable systems or otherwise unhealthy organization cultures. They discuss how important it is for the dominant culture to be responsive to the needs of minority cultures in their organizations and communities. They also address the need for members of the dominant culture to change values and behaviors as they move along the continuum of cultural competence toward cultural proficiency. Titles using these approaches include *A Peacock in the Land of Penguins* (Gallagher Hateley), *Courageous Conversations About Race* (Singleton), *Culturally Responsive Teaching* (Gay), and the many titles in Corwin's *Cultural Proficiency* collection.

This book is different. In this book, we speak to members of non-dominant cultures and provide them with tools for functioning effectively—or even thriving—in environments that are not yet ready or able to embrace them. Some books focus on changing the environment so that it is welcoming and inclusive to all people. This book focuses on helping those who are oppressed by their environments, because even the best of organizations will not be a comfortable fit for everyone. There will always be people who are marginalized or excluded because of who they are or the groups they belong to.

There are also people who perform the skills needed to do their job but do not fit well into the culture of their organization. This book will help them too. People who are systematically marginalized must learn strategies for fitting into where they are and protecting themselves from those who would target them. The goal, of course, is for everyone to change—to move from code switching by the non-dominant group, to code sharing by all members in the group, so that a mutually shared set of cultural expectations are cocreated.

There are many leaders who supervise people who don't quite fit into the organizational culture or who work with young people who don't fit, because they have not learned to code switch in an environment that is ill prepared to welcome them. This book provides strategies for helping marginalized people and those who work with them. This book also provides support for leaders who are working to transform the organization so it is a healthier place for all. This book will help people to

- Discern whether they are Fish Out of Water
- Recognize Fish Out of Water in their organizations
- Develop techniques for thriving in organizational cultures that don't quite fit
- Design strategies for creating and sustaining a healthy, inclusive organizational culture

THE POWER OF STORY

Storytelling is a powerful learning strategy. Through storytelling, people relate to, reflect upon, and learn from their lives and those who share their stories with them. Storytelling provides opportunities to bond and create community; it is also a powerful tool for creating empathy, facilitating healing, and inspiring action. The American idiom "like a Fish Out of Water" creates a colorful image of one who is an outsider or does not fit in. In all organizations or ponds or sophisticated indoor aquaria, there are those who are in the center of power and have great influence on the environment, and there are those who are marginalized and have very little influence. Throughout this book, we use the phrase *Fish Out of Water* as a shorthand description of the groups of people who do not fit into their environments. Those environments may be home, family, school, or a working environment. We tell stories about the many Fish Out of Water we have met and invite you to reflect on the Fish Out of Water you know or upon your own stories as someone who does not fit in.

Many people are Fish Out of Water because of their race, ethnicity, gender orientation, or because of their cognitive style, social style, or temperament. Others are Fish Out of Water because they have not learned, as a member of a non-dominant group, the codes or rules of the dominant culture. We lean heavily on the metaphor of finding a pond that fits or cleaning up the toxic waters so that the pond is safe for everyone, because our clients have found that this is a gentle way to enter into a tough conversation. Fish Out of Water symbolize the many people who are marginalized by or excluded from cultures—communities, systems, social groups—that are not large enough, diverse enough, or inclusive enough to welcome them to and keep them in the group.

Chimamandah Adichie reminds her audience in a 2009 TED talk that there is great danger in a single story. Holding a single story about self or others limits the nature of the relationships one might have. Throughout this book, we share our stories, the stories of our clients, and the stories of the many children who have crossed our paths. The stories are poignant, daunting, encouraging, and inspiring. We hope that you find wisdom in the stories we share and that you add your own as you explore what it means to be a Fish Out of Water.

One prevalent story about Fish Out of Water is that they need to be fixed—so they can be normal. We don't think so. Fish Out of Water need to be seen and heard—recognized for the diversity they add to whatever ponds they are swimming in. Those in the mainstream need to learn how to engage with these unique characters in ways that say, *I see you and I care.* And they need to clean up the ponds that are toxic for diverse schools of fish.

KIKANZA'S STORY

I was a Fish Out of Water in school. I was smart and got good grades. All the teachers liked me because I made them look good. Being a geek didn't make me a Fish Out of Water; because we were tracked in my high school, all of my classmates were geeks. However, that was not the case in gym. As comfortable as I was in the world of words and numbers, I was uncomfortable in gym class, because I was not a natural in sports. This was unfortunate, because my classmates and my teachers expected me to be.

I would watch the other Black girls fearlessly attack the balls in play. I would wring my hands anxiously as I watched the ball—as I was told to do. I would watch the ball . . . fall . . . roll past me . . . hit me in the stomach. But I never managed to catch it, throw it, or kick it anywhere it was supposed to go. So that meant when it was time to choose teams, I was the one who was chosen last. The team that didn't get me would laugh, and the team that did would groan. I was so bad with balls that for some games, like basketball, not even the coach wanted me to play because I spoiled the game for everyone else. "You be the referee," she would say. "You know all the rules." It is painful to remember being a Fish Out of Water in gym class.

It is easy to tell the stories of being smart and unathletic. It is harder to tell the stories of being excluded because I was a girl or because I was Black or because I wasn't Black enough. Later in life, I learned that I was a Fish Out of Water in more ways than I could have imagined—never quite being what was expected . . .

LEWIS' STORY

The early part of my educational journey was in segregated public schools in Little Rock, Arkansas, and I was a Fish Out of Water in my neighborhoods. My older sister attended Catholic school. She did so well that she was the type of student selected to be one of the high school kids who integrated Central High School in 1957. I was smart like my sister, but I couldn't risk acting smart among the neighborhood kids. Everyone on my street was cool; some were gang members (or wanna-bes). They expected me to be a poor student and to act like I was tough and dumb. To my sister's great displeasure, I acted like I was one of the street toughs, so I wouldn't get beat up by them or alienated from them. I excelled in school and eluded the tough kids, except for my fight with James Bones in sixth grade.

At the end of junior high school, my family moved to California. There, no one, particularly college counselors, expected the Black boy from the southern, segregated schools to do well. The disciplined home environment my sister had created for me and my siblings paid off. I enrolled in school just in time to take the national standard exams, called the Sputnik tests. I did so well, I was sent to special science and summer programs at Yale and Stanford, which totally ruined my reputation as a streetwise thug. However, neither of these personas were really me. I wasn't a geek; I wasn't a thug. I was a Fish Out of Water trying to fit in.

How This Book Is Organized

Having been Fish Out of Water most of our lives, we use our stories and those of our clients to illustrate the concepts we present. By telling their stories, people create places where previously invisible truths become visible (Coupland, 2014). As you read about what it means to be a Fish Out of Water, we invite you to think about your life and the stories you might tell about it. It is through the sharing of stories that people connect to one another, and it is through those connections that the foundation is laid for differences being understood, if not accepted, and for more people working to create safer, healthier environments in their communities and workplaces.

Each chapter includes stories about our clients and the work we do with them. There are stories about children and stories about adults, because Fish Out of Water come in all ages and a variety of settings. Some chapters focus on the people who don't fit in and other chapters focus on the people who manage, teach, or mentor them. At the end of the chapters are questions for reflection and storytelling in groups or personal journals and an informal assessment designed to deepen understanding of the concepts presented in the chapter. In the Resources section of the book are guidelines for a Book Study, and lists of videos, literature, and other materials that can be used for deepening your understanding of Fish Out of Water and the code sharing that makes the environmental ponds healthier for everyone.

GOING DEEPER

Reflect

- Tell of a time when you enjoyed someone telling you a story. How old were you?

- When and how have you used storytelling in your personal or professional life?

- Tell of a time when you used the process of storytelling to better understand a colleague or situation in the workplace.

1

Who Are the Fish Out of Water?

Fish Out of Water are people who are different because they do not know or meet the cultural expectations of their environments effectively. Many of these outsiders are simply people who don't know how to code switch. Others get targeted because they belong to groups that are unacceptable to the dominant culture; they are the outsiders who are pushed to the margins or who choose to walk there to avoid predators. In any organization or pond there are people on the margins, who may be invisible and voiceless to those who have greater influence in the environment.

ARE YOU A FISH OUT OF WATER?

Have you ever been someplace you thought you were supposed to be and wondered, "What am I doing here?" It could have been a social function or a conference, your job, or a family gathering . . . any place where you just didn't fit. You might have felt either completely invisible or hyper-visible.

No one paid any attention to you, or everyone wondered who let you in. This may be one of the patterns in your life, or it may have only occurred a couple of times.

When it happens, the emotional impact is the same: surprise and sometimes shock after realizing, no matter how warm the welcome, you just don't fit. Some people don't fit in at a couple of places; some people don't seem to fit anywhere. People who don't fit in are unable to make a contribution, because their discomfort, appearance, style, or background keeps them from being welcomed.

Children who are *Fish Out of Water* are often perceived by adults as needing to be fixed. They are labeled antisocial, odd, and different or viewed as snobbish and aloof. They may be Internet Introverts or Highly Sensitives. Emos, Geeks, and Nerds are also Fish Out of Water. While most people have had an experience, once or twice in their life-times, where they felt like a Fish Out of Water, some people feel like that every day. Others are quite comfortable with who they are but are perceived as undesirably different, or they belong to groups that are marginalized in a particular community, so they are treated as Fish Out of Water.

People without the temperament or social skills to respond adequately to aggressive communication styles and those who are introverts often get labeled as Fish Out of Water because they don't fit the norms of their extro-verted worlds. They may not be the only introverts in the environment, but because the culture is shaped for the extroverts, they feel alone and isolated. Cain suggests that extroversion is an enormously appealing personality style but has become an oppressive standard to which most people feel they must conform. "We get harassed by strang-ers, hounded by competitors, and asked intrusive ques-tions. We are the ones that take a dig, mull it over and spend days developing comebacks" (Cain, 2013, pp. 44–45).

It is unreasonable to expect all fish to fit everywhere, but, while there is a pond for every Fish Out of Water, every Fish won't fit into every pond. Unfortunately, Fish who are different get targeted. They become the victims of both

Aaron's Story

Aaron is a Fish Out of Water. He is a quiet boy being raised by his grandmother. Although he attends school with many children of color, he stands out in his clean but simple clothing and his restrained politeness. Aaron is deferential with all the adults he encounters; he rarely volunteers but is always responsive in the classroom. His teacher notices that he eats by himself in the cafeteria and usually arrives and leaves school alone. He doesn't seem to be clumsy but often is picking up his books from the hallway floor after bumping into someone or stumbling against a locker. When asked, Aaron said, "I don't feel safe in school. I try to stay out of the way but people pick on me. I didn't stumble; someone pushed me."

macro- and micro-aggressions. They get targeted because of the way they dress, the way they talk, the way they think, or the way they relate to people. Fish Out of Water are the people on the edges of the bell curve: They are too smart, too dumb, too fast, too slow, too fat, too tall, too short, too large, or too small. Fish Out of Water can be extremely attractive or very unattractive. Some school resource professionals use the term FLK—funny looking kid—for those who are marginalized and targeted as Fish Out of Water.

Fish Out of Water may be funny talkers or different thinkers. Their cognitive style may be abstract and random, while their organization's culture is concrete and sequential. They can be in the wrong-size pond or be a targeted species or just one of a few of their kind, for the pond they are in. Visionaries, without social skills, are Fish Out of Water. Paradigm Shifters, without patience, are Fish Out of Water. Truth Tellers, who can't keep quiet, are Fish Out of Water. Shadow Dwellers—people who are unseen and unheard by those in power—are Fish Out of Water.

SOME FISH OUT OF WATER KNOW THEY NEED TO LEAVE

One of the most gratifying aspects of our work is helping people who don't fit in understand why they are so miserable and helping them to leave places that don't work for them. An organization may request we work with one of their managers who brings a wealth of experience to the position, has excellent skills and does good work, but doesn't quite fit the cultural norms. We will help them to identify the unwritten rules of the organization and to recognize how important they are. We'll talk about what they need to do to fit in. It could be dress, style of presentation, or taking the time to socialize with the other managers. It is usually nothing directly related to the work but always something that affects the way the other workers perceive them.

With new understanding and renewed commitment, the client will work for a few weeks or months to change the way they engage with their colleagues. At the point when the internal conflict becomes too great a sacrifice for them, they decide to leave. While leaving is never the goal of these interventions, it often is best for the individual and the organization. The person leaving has additional skills for discerning whether an organization's culture is suitable for them. The organization can better describe its culture and the characteristics of the people who will be most successful in that environment.

It is possible for people to thrive in oppressive or uncomfortable organizational climates, if they have skills that help them to adapt to the culture of the

Shari's Story

Shari worked for one of the largest publishing houses in the United States. "She is the best editor I have ever known," said her boss. But she didn't fit in the publishing company. Shari is an unreformed, unapologetic, unreconstructed hippie. She is over sixty, and she still wears Birkenstocks, tie-dye T-shirts, and her hair in two long braids. She absolutely refused to change anything about how she looked, so thirty years ago she walked away from a promising career because she didn't fit in. She was conscious of her incompetence in that organizational culture. Fortunately, she was able to create a professional life that has worked for her outside of a corporate structure. But it is as clear to us now as it was to us then, Shari is a Fish Out of Water.

organization they are in. Swimming in toxic waters is not an ideal situation but may be a necessary survival strategy for Fish Out of Water. In the worst cases, they should be encouraged to leave for safer ponds.

SOME FISH OUT OF WATER DON'T KNOW THEY DON'T FIT IN

Everyone feels out of place at some time in his or her life, and most people have a pond—or two—where they are welcomed and the ecosystem suits them. They leave their ponds occasionally because they want to—they just need a break. For the most part, the pond, the people in it, and the work they do there, feels pretty comfortable.

Are You in the Right Pond?

You know you belong because it feels right; you are affirmed by the people around you. Your internal radar tells you it's right. How's it feeling?

Many Fish Out of Water are not that fortunate. They haven't learned to respond appropriately to the cultural expectations of their environment. This unconscious cultural incompetence results in unpleasant surprises. They don't fit in, and they feel stuck. They don't fit in, and they don't know why. Or worse, they don't fit in and don't even realize they don't fit. They get poor performance appraisals. They get passed over for promotion. They get complaints filed against them, or people just work around them. They don't get invited out to lunch or to other social functions. Meetings get held, and they are not included; decisions get made, and they are not consulted. They are Fish Out of Water and don't even know it.

Children who are Fish Out of Water may have learned to deny or dismiss the cues that let them know something is wrong. They may not complain, but like Aaron, they know that they don't fit in. Some are comfortable sitting on the edges of their groups; others long to belong. "Maslow had it wrong," says social neuroscientist Matthew Lieberman. "Being socially connected and cared for is paramount. Without social support, infants will never survive to become adults who can provide for themselves. . . . Love and belonging might seem like a convenience we can live without, but our biology is built to thirst for connection . . . our need for connection is bedrock." (Lieberman, 2013, p. 43) Whether or not they complain, whether or not they know there is a problem, Fish Out of Water are people who are different because they do not know the cultural expectations of their environments or cannot respond to those expectations effectively. These people get targeted because they are different; they are the outsiders because of the groups to which they belong, or they are outsiders because they are too different from the members of their group. Being an outsider is heartbreakingly painful to many people because of the intense human need for social connection (Lieberman, 2013, p. 48). What helps people to stay connected and at the same time may target or marginalize others is cultural codes.

LEARNING TO PLAY THE GAME

Code switching is a sociolinguistic term that refers to shifting one's language and style of discourse to match the social expectations. Most people are familiar with the code switching required of someone who speaks more than one language. Fewer people are conscious of the code switching that occurs throughout the day as people shift their styles when talking to social peers or superiors. Code switching also occurs when shifting from a formal to a more casual conversation. In addition to these commonly learned styles of code switching, subtler code switching demands are made of people as they move from one organizational culture to another.

People learn to code switch early in life. Children who easily change their mode of engagement as they seek favors from a sibling or a parent give evidence to this phenomenon. Their style matches the mode and expectations of the person with whom they engage. By the time they complete elementary school, most children have learned to authentically represent themselves while adjusting to the demands or subtler requirements of different teachers.

The people whom we call Fish Out of Water are the ones who are unaware of the need to code switch and the people—children and adults—who do not code switch effectively. They may use the same codes all the time. Consequently, there are places where their behavior and language is appropriate and, unfortunately, many places where they just do not fit in. Another way to understand code switching and the process of decoding or learning the codes of a culture is to think of the social interaction within a group as a game.

Whenever you play a game, you must learn the rules. The basic rules remain the same wherever and with whomever you play. Rules differ as you move from one player to another or to different social contexts.

Charla's Story

Charla is a brilliant student who is taking advanced placement courses in physics, English, and history. She is a competitive swimmer who starts training in the wee hours of the morning. She is also from a working-class African American community. She is tolerated but not fully accepted by her swimming teammates, who are mostly White and high income. She also has a hard time with other Black students, since there are not many in her classes or on the swim team. She is challenged by everyone for being too different. Because she is a talented painter as well, Charla finds solace with her art, but she is lonely. . . . Artist, scientist, athlete, Charla has learned the codes of several different environments but has not found an environment where she feels comfortable. She is a Fish Out of Water because, even though she excels, she hasn't found a place where she is comfortable and accepted.

Basketball involves moving the ball from one end of the court to the other and getting it though the hoop. The rules change with the context: a child playing with an older sibling in the driveway, friends playing against one another at the court in the neighborhood park, college students playing in a tournament, professional ball players at a municipal arena. Whatever the game—even solitaire on the computer—adjustments are made by the players when the context for playing changes.

CIRCUMSTANTIAL AND PERPETUAL FISH OUT OF WATER

Some people are Fish Out of Water in a particular environment; some people are Fish Out of Water all the time. People who don't fit into social groups, schools, organizations, or their families can develop adaptive skills so that they can survive in a pond that is not of their choosing. Knowing how to code switch will be helpful to these Fish Out of Water; however, they may always feel out of place until they find the right pond. When an environment is not committed to being both diverse and inclusive, Fish Out of Water rarely thrive.

Some groups in American society have been historically marginalized. Immigrants, minority ethnic groups, women, the differently abled, members of the LGBTQi communities, poor people, and youth have throughout history been the targets of discrimination, injustice, and marginalization by the dominant culture. From a historical perspective, members of these groups are perpetual Fish Out of Water. Within these groups are people who know how to code switch and are successful within and outside of their native groups. Others in these groups are frustrated and struggling, invisible, voiceless, on the margins, or outside looking into a culture that is toxic for them.

There are also people who are perceived as odd, who may or may not belong to the groups that have been historically marginalized. They are Fish Out of Water and are productive, functional, and satisfied; their ecosystem works for them. There are others—people who are different and who are unconscious of their differentness or unwilling or unable to do differently. There are very few places where these people fit in. Among them, some want help, others don't. This book addresses the issues of the odd, dysfunctional, or dissatisfied Fish Out of Water—circumstantial or perpetual—who want help, and the people who teach, supervise, and worry about them.

GOING DEEPER

Reflect

- Tell a story about being a Fish Out of Water or being with one.

Assess

Are You a Fish Out of Water?
Focusing on a particular environment, answer the following questions. After you have answered these questions, discuss your responses with someone you trust, who knows you well.

1. Can you swim wherever you want to in your pond?

2. Do you think you are different from others in your group? How are you different?

3. Do people make comments about how different you are?

4. Do you choose to be different? Why do you make those choices?

5. Do you know if you fit in?

6. Do you look like the people around you? How do you differ?

7. Do you speak or behave like the people in your environment? How do you differ?

8. Do you wonder what the rules are to be successful in your environment? How do you know?

9. Do you stay close to the margins? Why?

10. Do you know how to influence the insiders?

11. Do you know who the predators are in your environment?

12. Can you protect yourself from predators?

13. Can you engage with both the outsiders and insiders effectively?

14. Do you know and understand the cultural expectations of your environment?

15. Are you thriving in your environment? What would keep you from struggling or surviving?

16. Do you feel offended, constrained, or restricted by the organization's norms?

17. Do you feel voiceless, invisible, or powerless in your environment?

18. Do people have problems with you because you are different? What kind of problems do people have with you?

19. Do these differences make a difference?

20. Is there another environment (or pond) where you do fit? How does it differ from the one you focused on?

Discuss

Using a pond or tank as the metaphor, draw yourself in the environment of your organization:

- Describe the nature of diversity.
- Illustrate how well people fit in the environment.
- Identify dangerous areas, support places, obstacles, and opportunities.
- Depict toxic or marginalizing practices, policies, or personnel.
- Draw yourself.

2

What Is Code Switching?

Code switching is a sociolinguistic term that refers to the process of changing one's style of communication to suit the socio/politico/cultural context of the exchange. While often used when describing the use of language by people who speak two different languages, the term also describes the adjustments a speaker makes when moving from one social context to another. When code switching, the nonverbal aspects of the communication event—body language, attire, and attitude—also may change. Code switching involves learning to engage according to the unwritten rules of the environment's culture. *Code Sharing* is a necessary skill in a Culturally Proficient environment.

When people learn how to play games, whether the games are cards, dodgeball, or chess, there are standard rules that are followed—wherever the game is played—and there are house rules. House rules are set by the dominant culture—the host of the game or perhaps the home team or the players who use the field regularly.

To play the game well, the others must learn the additional rules and discern if and how the standard rules are being used. Code switching means playing the game according to the rules that have been set by the home team—or the dominant group—while temporarily suspending or adjusting the rules one may have learned natively. If life is a game and cultural codes are the rules that govern the game, then code switching is the use of the rules in a way that insures a person can play to win. Playing to win means that a person has learned the rules of the environments in which she functions and switches from one set of codes to another with ease, accuracy, and appropriateness.

Code switching is a human skill that is natural to all, especially the young. Watch a two-year-old walk into a room. The child can determine, almost immediately, how to get what he needs and wants from each adult in the household and the various children present. Each person may have a slightly different set of rules. Mothers respond to crying or whimpering, while fathers may be quicker to respond to fear and laughter. Siblings tease, protect, and collude with one another, and each act comes with a complex set of codes that varies from family to family. People who are skilled at moving from one environment to another successfully have learned to code switch. People who code switch well have learned to discern that new rules are in force and what those new rules are.

Many Fish Out of Water do not know how to code switch or that they need to. Hazel had been on her job for fifteen years when the new CEO and the HR director decided that if Hazel did not develop better interpersonal skills she would lose her job.

"I don't understand what they want," Hazel complained to her coach. "I have met all of the financial goals of the department. We have increased our profit margin every year. I hire good people to work for us."

This was all true. However, what the executive team wanted was for Hazel to build team loyalty and camaraderie. They wanted fewer turnovers in the department. They wanted Hazel to come out of her silo and work with her colleagues in the other departments—sharing information and ideas that would benefit the company.

After several conversations with Hazel and the executive managers, the coach discovered that Hazel, who had immigrated to the United States from China when she was in college, had mastered formal American English language but had not learned to code switch from formal to casual or less formal styles of English. She always spoke very formally, which was off-putting to some of her colleagues. She was submissive to her boss and she ignored her staff. She did not engage with other departments because she did not want to bother anyone or have anyone think she could not do her job. She brought to work her Chinese cultural norms. Her colleagues thought she had no people skills, when actually she was using the people skills appropriate to her native Chinese culture. She did not know how to translate her relationship paradigms from her native culture to her present situation. She did not even know there was a difference.

Code switching is not dualism—that is, assimilating so well into one group that the group members have no idea that the person may belong to another cultural group. Code switching is not learning to engage inauthentically with people in power. Code switching is a Culturally Proficient practice; it is a display of intercultural competence. It is a tactic or skill that allows one to function in two (or more) cultures. This does not imply that one subjugates his native codes to a dominant culture, rather, that one understands the rules of both and can use those rules/codes appropriately. The native codes are supplemented with the codes of second and subsequent cultures.

SOFIA'S STORY

Sofia spoke English with a flawless American accent. She never spoke Spanish around her college friend Savannah because she assumed Savannah didn't know any Spanish.

Because English was the dominant, or alpha, language, it was the privilege of Sofia's friends to not ask if she spoke another language. Consequently, a good part of her (self, culture, worldview) was hidden from her friends. She supplemented her first language with a second. She was truly bicultural—Sofie in one world, Sofia in the other. She did not assimilate; she did not supplant her first culture, replacing it with the second. As a minority person, she was forced to function in two cultures without much crossover. Her English-speaking friends missed the opportunity to use their Spanish, if they had any, and to learn some of the codes of Sofia's culture. Sofia's code switching skills enabled her to acculturate to the dominant group.

Why Code Switch?

While it is possible to move through life using the few codes learned in childhood, members of historically marginalized groups learn to code switch in order to survive in the dominant culture. These native codes do not protect children from being targeted by their teachers for not knowing the code of school or for not learning the particular codes of their classroom. Knowing only their native codes does not protect children from being bullied or provide adults with the relationship skills needed to be successful at work.

In an ideal world, the dominant group will adapt to the differences of minority groups among them. Both the dominant and non-dominant groups will learn from one another the codes appropriate for successful communication. Ultimately, through this code sharing, a third set of codes that all members in the diverse group use and understand will be developed. Unfortunately, there are few places where this utopian communication exists. Consequently, in order to be heard, seen, and included, Fish Out of Water must learn the codes of the ponds in which they swim. Once they learn the codes for effective communication in their particular environment, they are better able to advocate for equity and justice. Those who work with, manage, teach, and mentor Fish Out of Water can do better in those roles if they code share with the Fish Out of Water rather than relying solely on their ability to code switch.

At a professional development session, Dewey was fielding questions and comments from the class. Blaine, a veteran teacher who came of age during the Civil Rights Movement, said, "I thought Cultural Proficiency was about changing systems. Fish Out of Water are the oppressed; we aren't supposed to change them. That's assimilationist."

"Yes," Dewey responded. "We are trying to change systems, and we are trying to help people adapt and adjust to new environments. When you make the commitment to diversity and inclusion everyone changes. No matter how good a dancer you might be, when you dance with a new partner your style changes a bit. To be able to dance with anyone, you must learn the steps that your partners use. If you insist on dancing in a ballroom, you need to know the basic ballroom steps, just as anyone who jumps up on a hip hop stage is expected to move in a way that approximates The Krump or The Wobble. It is not assimilation; it is appropriate code switching."

Delores, a first-year teacher who was struggling to succeed in the unfamiliar suburban environment, said, "I thought Cultural Proficiency meant I didn't have to change. The dominant culture is supposed to make room for me."

"Yes, Dee," Dewey replied. "The Cultural Proficiency journey means making room at the table for everyone who wants a seat and needs a voice. But if you are not in charge of the table, then you are going to have to learn the language of those who are—so they can understand you. So they can learn from you.

"And just as you are challenged to learn their codes, they are challenged to learn yours. If you are not a part of the dominant group, unfortunately, at least in this culturally precompetent state, you bear the greater responsibility of learning the codes of the dominant culture. You are expanding your cultural repertoire by learning their codes. In time, with everyone open to learning and growing, everyone will code share."

"Oh, I get it," Blaine said. "When you are in the dominant culture the squeaky wheel gets the grease. When you are a minority, the nail that sticks up gets pounded down."

CODE SWITCHING IN SCHOOLS

In schools, educators speak of the hidden curriculum. All students must learn to read, write, speak, compute, and use technology, and yet, this is not all they must learn. In order to be successful, they must learn to *do school* appropriately. They must know the codes and play by the codes, the set of rules, established by educators—the dominant group. Additionally, children must learn the codes of their peer groups and learn to switch accordingly. Failure to learn these codes results in the student being targeted and punished by the educators and targeted, bullied, or ostracized by peer groups.

The rules of school or the hidden curriculum are extensive in number and complex in nature. There are critical, nonacademic things that students must learn:

- The difference between an inside voice and an outside voice and when each is appropriate
- The kind of touching that is appropriate
- When it is OK to roughhouse
- The different consequences for hitting someone at home or at school
- That touching the private areas of one's body or anyone else's is not OK—neither is talking about them
- How to sit for long periods of time at tables or on the floor in positions that may be unfamiliar or uncomfortable for growing bodies
- That the consequences for disrespecting another's personal property as well as the definition of such may be much more severe than at home

This list is just the beginning. After learning to read the signals of their bodies and to control their bladders, students are then required to ask permission to use the toilet and to wait until it is time. Adults are not the majority culture of the school environment, but they are the dominant culture.

They set the rules. Adults must be addressed with deference and in a particular way. Students may come from homes where adults are addressed by their first names. In schools, all adults are addressed by a title and their last names, except perhaps the coach or the custodians—who may not be addressed at all.

Most difficult for children are the school rules that contrast with the home rules. When they go to school, children must learn to organize themselves into lines, separated by gender. They may have learned to say "excuse me," to ask for permission to talk when others are talking at home. At school they learn to raise their hands and wait until they are called upon. At home, most of the time, a new topic of conversation can be introduced. At school, students must learn to limit their comments to the topic that has been established by the teacher. At home, a child may have been called by a nickname, but at school, the child might be forced to respond to a name that while legal may be totally unfamiliar to him.

Every culture has rules. Teachers who have difficulty with children whom they perceive as willfully noncompliant often don't recognize that their students are playing by a different set of rules. These rules may reflect the roles they have at home as oldest child responsible for younger siblings or being *the man of the house*. The codes used by

---

A Name Story

Stanley was delighted that his younger brother, Charles, was finally old enough to attend school with him. Stanley's job was to walk his brother to school and back home again and to look out for him during school. He was confused when his teacher released him at the end of the first day by saying, "You may go pick up Maurice; he is waiting for you in his classroom."

"Who is Maurice?" Stanley asked, puzzled.

"He's your brother, of course," the teacher responded.

"I don't have a brother named Maurice. My brother's name is Charles."

After a bit more conversation and a walk to the classroom where Maurice Charles was waiting for his older brother, Stanley learned that the brother he had known all of his life had two names! A family name and a school name.

children that may be perceived as defiant self-confidence may be the bravado that enables a child to navigate safely the route between home and school.

Codes are also developed by children. These codes determine friendship groups and standards for dress—within the guidelines set by the adults in their worlds or in opposition to them. There are codes that reflect what is acceptable to eat by the different groups. Some groups may bring their lunches; other groups may only buy lunch in the cafeteria. Others must eat from the vending machines in the school in order to be accepted by their peers. There are rules about clothes, shoes, attitudes toward homework, and more. To be successful in school, children must learn to navigate within this complex system of rules set by the dominant group and the subgroups to which they may belong.

CODE SWITCHING AS ADULTS

The codes for adults are subtler and just as important. Kathy worked at Apple for several years. Then she decided that she needed to experience another technological perspective, so she switched to IBM. "I'm bilingual!" she declared. She was more correct than she knew. In order to thrive at these two very different technological giants, Kathy had to learn not only the differences between the two operating systems but also the differences in the corporate cultures. To the casual outsider, Apple was T-shirts and jeans, while IBM was pumps and pearls. But the differences were deeper than attire. The operating systems and the expected attire were manifestations of the cultural expectations, the nature of communication, and other norms of the cultures. Not everyone figured this out.

While Kathy was at Apple, Joshua, the dean of the school of education of one of the major universities in the area, was hired. He had the skills and information to help Apple meet its goals for technology and education; however, he did not code switch well. Instead of seeking to learn how things were done at Apple, he took his university cultural norms with him; he even insisted on wearing his tweed jacket and slacks on casual Fridays. For Joshua, casual meant no ties, not shorts and flip-flops. Clothing had nothing to do with the talent he brought to the job, but it gravely impacted the relationships he needed to get the job done, because the Apple staff perceived him as unapproachable. Had he done what he perceived to be superficial code switching, he might have learned the cultural codes that were most important to his success at Apple. Instead, he returned to the university. Kathy learned the codes and used them. Joshua noticed the codes but did not recognize how important they were.

Some people believe that using the code of another group, in which they may be marginalized or overtly oppressed, is an expression of disloyalty to one's native group and an inauthentic expression of self. Some think using the codes of the non-dominant group is cultural appropriation—a form of disrespect. This perspective is manifest in the controversy around the names of athletic teams or in the acclamation, "My culture is not your costume." Others understand that code switching is another form of bilingualism; it is an aspect of being bicultural. A good code switcher can switch between cultures in a manner that is comfortable for all involved in the interaction. Yet for those who are not as culturally versatile, the differences in behaviors may be confusing.

A well-dressed Black man spoke elegantly to an audience of college professors. After the session, he engaged with his colleagues, at Latimer College, in the same articulate, soft-spoken manner. Some time later, he was seen talking at a neighborhood basketball court where Black and Hispanic men were involved in a pick-up game. It was hard to believe he was the same person; his gait was different, and his voice was louder, high pitched, and punctuated with laughter as he greeted the ball players with complex handshakes. He knew the codes of two, very different, cultural groups.

WHO MAKES THE RULES?

It is clear to most observers which is the dominant culture and consequently which group can claim the right to set the norms for the organization. Most formal leaders are a part of the dominant group—at home it is the parents; in school it is the administrators; in other organizations it is the senior managers. There are times, however, when the nonformal leaders shape the culture. Laila learned this in a very painful way. Laila was a new principal at Du Bois Middle School. She had been successful as a vice principal and was looking forward to being in charge at her new school. She had notes, lists, and lessons learned from her last school. Since graduate school, Laila had a vision of what her school would be like with herself leading the way. She hit the ground running with change, focusing on how things ought to be at her ideal school. She engaged with her teachers with pleasant, encouraging, one-way conversations about her standards. She chastised teachers for not using the strategies she recommended. "I have to get these scores up," she told them. Seasoned teachers pushed back because they felt they were being told they were wrong, not being acknowledged for their experience and not being asked for opinions or offered options.

Laila felt it was her right and responsibility to tell the teachers what to do and did not alter her tactics. Most of the faculty had been teaching for longer than Laila had been an administrator. All of the teachers had been at the school and in the community longer than Laila had been there. They knew the parents, and they knew their union leaders. The codes Laila used for making organizational change were unacceptable to the teachers, and they rebelled. Through parent complaints and union sanctions, they let Laila know they were not going to change. Laila was forced out of her job and out of the district. She thought, as principal, she was in charge; she learned that, at least at Du Bois, the teachers ran the school and she did not know how to talk with them.

Nonverbal Code Switching

Code switching occurs overtly and on subtle levels within a culture. There are codes about appropriate dress, body language, intergender and cross-gender interaction, language style, syntax, and lexicon. There are codes about how one engages with others in the group and codes for the same interactions with people outside of one's group. Nonverbal codes are the most complex and are often misused. Appropriate code switching requires an understanding of the subtext of the cultural exchange. Switching between languages may result in an accent or incorrect pronunciation or intonation. Switching cultural codes by mimicking what one sees may result in an inauthentic expression that further isolates the person from the people with whom he seeks to connect.

Peter, who was Dean of Advancement at Latimer, a small liberal arts college in California, had learned that Black people use a more complicated ritual for handshaking than White people, like himself. He was taught the handshake and used it successfully with his Black male golf buddies. He was proud to have learned the codes of greeting and saying goodbye in an African American community. At an alumni gathering, he met Aliyah, a Black woman, whom he admired greatly, and after establishing a collegial relationship of mutual regard, he sought to show her that he knew some of the codes of her community. He was puzzled by her response when he attempted to use the fancy handshake ritual. She kept her hands at her side and simply said, "I don't do that." Later, after she reflected on what had happened, she explained to Peter that while he had learned some of the code, he had not learned it all. The ritual was exclusive to men; women didn't shake hands that way. Moreover, he must be careful not to initiate the handshake but to wait until he was invited to use it with other Black men.

Kenneth R. Johnson, a Black American sociolinguist, was among the first to describe the kinesics codes of African

Americans (Johnson, 1971, pp. 181–189). As U.S. urban culture has become more visible, the codes have become more complex. There are codes for every major ethnic group in U.S. cities and codes for the groups within them. For example, within a city, there are codes that distinguish differences between hip hop, gang, metrosexual, and gender nonconforming cultures that also have distinctive rules for the many ethnic groups that are members of these cultures. The use of codes helps to identify who is in which groups.

Code Switching Is a Life Skill

Each group has its own rules. For a diverse organization to become inclusive, both dominant and non-dominant groups must develop and enhance their code switching skills. They must teach their codes to those who don't know them and learn the codes of others. Dominant groups are morally obligated to do this. When newcomers arrive at their house, they must teach the house rules. Problems occur when it is assumed that everyone knows what the rules are. When the prevalent belief is that *everybody knows* what is *common sense*, Fish Out of Water are punished for not using the codes that no one has taught them.

After Hazel worked with her coach for a few months, she began to recognize the codes she had been missing. She grew more adept at code switching and everyone—her boss, the HR director, even her husband, complimented her on the change. Peter was very grateful to his friend for explaining the subtler codes of shaking hands with African Americans. He continued to deepen his relationships and was perceived as sincere and authentic as he learned to code switch among Black Americans. Kathy's natural ability to learn codes and code switch appropriately enabled her to have adventures at Apple, IBM, Microsoft, and school districts large and small, urban and suburban. Stanley and Maurice Charles had their first lesson in code switching early in life. This opened them to noticing and learning more codes as they progressed in school and life.

Code switching may be perceived as politically correct behavior because it is acceding to the rules of the alphas in the environment. Culturally proficient code switching for the dominant culture means learning the values and adapting to the needs of those in the group who are not part of the dominant culture. For non-dominant groups, code switching means learning the codes of those in power and using them effectively. To choose not to code switch is to choose to be criticized and perhaps marginalized by those who do. Learning to code switch opens doors and opportunities for lifelong learning. Code sharing—when both dominant and non-dominant groups learn new codes—is the ultimate goal.

GOING DEEPER

Reflect

- How, in a typical day, are you called to code switch?
- How often do you switch codes?

Assess

Are You Aware of the Codes in Your Environment?
Focusing on one particular environment, describe the dominant culture and its members by answering these questions.

1. What are the opportunities for code switching?

2. Who have you noticed code switches well?

3. Who knows your codes?

4. What other codes do they know that you know of?

5. Who is marginalized because of unsuccessful code switching?

6. What happens when the codes are violated?

7. What codes don't you know that would be useful to know?

8. What are the codes for success in this environment?

9. Who is proficient in code switching?

10. Who needs coaching in code switching?

Discuss

- Tell of a time when you (or someone you were observing) code switched comfortably and with surprising ease.
- Tell of a time when you thought you were code switching but did it unsuccessfully.

3

What Is Cultural Proficiency?

The four components of the Cultural Proficiency Framework are the Guiding Principles, the Continuum, the Barriers, and the Essential Elements. The principles are the foundation of the framework; they describe the values necessary for understanding and working effectively with Fish Out of Water. The Continuum illustrates the steps along the way from a highly toxic environment to a deeply gratifying and mutually rewarding one. The Barriers explain why the Cultural Proficiency journey is a difficult one. They help to explain how someone is pushed to the edges or out of the water. The Essential Elements are used to outline the steps for teaching people to code switch and for making the school climate or organizational environment healthy for diverse populations.

WHY WORK FOR DIVERSITY AND INCLUSION?

There are many reasons for working to create a diverse and inclusive organizational climate. Diversity within means better customer service. If the people within the organization are familiar with groups that are different from them, they will be more understanding, empathetic, and appropriate in delivering their service or product to others. Working with a diverse group of people means that all present will be in a richer, more fertile environment. Individuals will be inspired, challenged, and supported; managers will have the benefit of people contributing to the work product with a variety of viewpoints, experiences, and styles. In a diverse and inclusive workplace the people in the system, at some point, will be encouraged to stretch outside of their comfort zone. They will be invited to grow as they learn from the differences in their environment.

These are tremendous benefits, and they don't come easily. To benefit from a diverse and inclusive environment, every member in the system must learn to recognize the differences that make a difference, value diversity, adapt to it, and manage the dynamics of difference. It is much easier to support a system where everyone looks alike, thinks alike, and acts alike. This is done by pushing the Fish who don't fit to the edges of the pond or completely out of the water. Fish Out of Water may be excluded, marginalized, or exterminated when they don't conform to the culture of their ponds.

WHAT IS CULTURE?

Culture is the water in which people swim. When you swim in the same waters all the time, with others who are just like you, there is no need to talk about the culture or the rules that govern it. Everybody knows them. It is only when the culture changes or the people within the organization's culture begin to change or diversify that people start to notice that some of those new people—those others—are not abiding by the rules, the ones that every one ought to know. No living being, human or animal, is without culture, which is why when you are an alpha in your own culture, you don't notice it.

Culture is the set of beliefs and practices shared by a group that give meaning to the interactions and identity of the members of the group. Membership in a culture is tied to one's affinity with the group and to the group's perception of who its members are. The rules that govern a culture, the cultural expectations, are called the codes. Some of the codes are explicitly taught; others are unstated, not even implicit—for example, the rule about the unmarked parking space that is always saved for the principal or the rules about who sits where in the teachers' lunchroom. In schools, these codes are called the hidden curriculum; in organizations they might be called the unwritten rules. People learn them through mentoring, observation, and by making mistakes.

Culture is a term that often is used in place of *race* and *ethnicity*. *Cultural diversity* is the phrase used, customarily, to indicate that people of color are present in a group. In this book, we use the term *culture* to mean this and more. A *cultural group* is a community of people united in beliefs and practice. Every person belongs to several cultural groups. One's race and ethnicity may define one of those groups; gender orientation, language, and geography may delineate others. Other significant cultural groups include entrepreneurs, artists, and educators. Each group has experiences and mindsets that provide a particular lens for understanding and experiencing the world. Socioeconomic markers, such as wealth, income, education, and leisure activities also contribute to one's culture. When the boundaries of several cultural groups overlap, a community that shares several unifying identifiers exists, often as the primary culture for its members. For example, straight, White, middle class, Protestant men and women from urban suburbs, on the coasts of the United States, share many beliefs, values, and lifestyle practices in common. Theirs is a culture.

THE CULTURAL PROFICIENCY FRAMEWORK

Both people and organizations are identified by their cultures. *Cultural Proficiency* is an approach to learning about, living productively among, and working effectively with people and within organizations that have cultural expectations that differ from yours. Cultural Proficiency involves both individual behaviors and organizational practices: It is the values and behaviors of individuals and the policies and practices for institutions that insure healthy, productive, inclusive interactions with colleagues, clients, and community. The Cultural Proficiency Framework was presented for the first time, in a monograph by Terry Cross and his colleagues (1989). The components of the Framework include the following:

- **Values** that are the foundation of the approach
- **Language** for describing productive and destructive behaviors and situations
- **Attitudes** and **systems** that undermine movement toward Cultural Proficiency
- **Standards** for planning, evaluating, and developing policies, programs, and interactions

What makes Culturally Proficient behavior a challenge to describe is that it is not precise; it is ambiguous and contextualized. Similar to sexual harassment, what is appropriate in one environment may be highly inappropriate in another—for example, behavior that is appropriate and welcome at a party may be highly inappropriate in the office. To be Culturally Proficient you have to assess the environment and determine the cultural expectations for that particular setting. To be a diverse and inclusive organization means that you share the cultural expectations with newcomers, instead of waiting for them to figure them out, or teach people, instead of punishing them because they don't know the rules of the environment. The goal of the Cultural Proficiency journey is for members of both dominant and non-dominant groups—alphas and betas—to learn, to teach, and to use the codes—the cultural expectations of their cultures—with one another.

In his seminal work, Terry Cross introduces the term *Cultural Competence*. The term's alliterative qualities make it attractive, and today it is used ubiquitously; many don't realize that it refers to this specific framework presented by Cross. As consultants, when we approached communities of color about becoming Culturally Competent, we were often told that as people of color, they were already Culturally Competent and didn't need to learn anything more. We responded with an affirmation, "Yes, you may be Culturally Competent," and a challenge, "but are you Culturally Proficient?" Because Cultural Proficiency is the ultimate point on the Cultural Proficiency Continuum, as authors and consultants, we have chosen to use it when referring to the Cross framework.

The chart in Figure 3.1 summarizes the Cultural Proficiency Framework as presented by Terry Cross (1989).

THE GUIDING PRINCIPLES OF CULTURAL PROFICIENCY

The **Principles** are the values that must underlie the work of anyone on the Cultural Proficiency journey.

- *Culture is a predominant force.* Everything is affected by culture—yours and others'. It is also impossible to be culturally neutral or unbiased. If you are unaware of your culture or the codes in your cultural milieu, you are most likely in the dominant culture.
- *People are served in varying degrees by the dominant culture.* The codes of the dominant culture are designed to serve that group and to keep it dominant. Only as Fish Out of Water learn the codes of the dominant culture can they improve the likelihood of their survival in an unwelcoming culture and move toward thriving in it.

Figure 3.1 The Components of the Cultural Proficiency Framework

Cultural Proficiency is the policies and practices in an organization or the values and behavior of an individual that enable the person or institution to engage effectively with people and groups who are different from them. Cultural Proficiency is an inside-out approach that influences how people relate to their colleagues, clients, and community. The Framework has four components: The Guiding Principles, the Continuum, the Barriers, and the Essential Elements.

THE GUIDING PRINCIPLES

The Principles are the foundational values on which the framework is built.

- Culture is a predominant force.
- People are served in varying degrees by the dominant culture.
- There is diversity within and between cultures.
- Every group has culturally defined needs.
- People have personal identities and group identities.
- Marginalized groups have to be at least bicultural.
- Each group's culture influences how problems are defined and solved.
- Families, as defined by their cultures, are the primary systems of support.

THE CULTURAL PROFICIENCY CONTINUUM

The Continuum provides language for describing situations and events.

CULTURAL DESTRUCTION	CULTURAL INTOLERANCE	CULTURAL REDUCTIONISM	CULTURAL PRE-COMPETENCE	CULTURAL COMPETENCE	CULTURAL PROFICIENCY
Destroy differences. Judge differences among people as wrong and seek to eliminate them.	Demean differences. Accept that differences exist, but regard some as superior to others.	Discount differences. Act as if there are no differences. Treat everyone equally, regardless of their differences.	Accommodate differences. Begin to make changes, some of which may be inadequate or incorrect because of limited understanding.	Collaborate with differences. Use the Essential Elements as standards for individual behavior and organizational practices.	Cocreate a healthy environment. Advocate for and learn from differences.

THE BARRIERS TO CULTURAL PROFICIENCY

The Barriers are systems and attitudes that undermine the Cultural Proficiency journey.

- Unawareness of the need to adapt
- Resistance to change
- Institutionalized systems of oppression and privilege
- A sense of entitlement
- Misuse and abuse of the power that accompanies privilege

THE ESSENTIAL ELEMENTS

The Elements provide standards for planning and evaluating.

- **Assess Culture**
  Identify the groups present in the system and the norms and expectations of the cultural environment.
- **Value Diversity**
  Demonstrate an appreciation for the differences among and between groups.
- **Manage the Dynamics of Difference**
  Respond appropriately and effectively to the issues that arise in a diverse environment.
- **Adapt to Diversity**
  Change policies and adopt new behaviors and practices that eliminate inequities.
- **Institutionalize Cultural Knowledge**
  Drive the changes into the systems of the organization and advocate for those who may not have access to the privileges of the dominant groups.

- *There is diversity within and between cultures.* Groups are not monolithic; everyone in a group may appear to be the same, but there will be discernible differences among them. Within racial-ethnic groups, for example, there are marked class differences.
- *Every group has unique culturally defined needs.* It is not the responsibility of the dominant culture to meet all of these needs, but it is necessary that the needs be acknowledged and respected. These needs may affect decisions in such things as grooming, attire, dietary restrictions, and holidays.
- *People have personal identities and group identities.* People want to be recognized as individuals as well as members of their groups. Both identities are important. It is usually not received as a compliment when a child is told he is different from his family or his racial-ethnic group.
- *Marginalized populations have to be at least bicultural to be successful.* Beta groups must learn the codes of both their cultures and the dominant cultures with which they interact. Alpha groups can be successful in the dominant culture knowing only their own codes.
- *Families, as defined by their cultures, are the primary systems of support.* A family may not be a biological unit, so it is important to notice idiosyncratic and cultural differences in how families are defined.
- *Each group's culture influences how problems are defined and solved.* What is perceived to be a problem will differ from one group to another, so it is important not to presume that all parties involved deem a situation to be problematic.

THE CULTURAL PROFICIENCY CONTINUUM

The Continuum provides language for describing polices, practices, situations, and events. Asking, "Where would you place that policy on the Continuum?" may open the door to a deeper conversation about the usefulness or appropriateness of an action. Cultural Proficiency is a journey; very few if any people are consistently at the far end of the Continuum in all of their beliefs and practices. You are only as proficient as your last conversation. You might be excellent in navigating the LGBTQi community and pretty good at engaging with people who speak your language and are of different ethnic groups. You may, however, find gender equity to be difficult for you because of your upbringing, or you may experience extreme dissonance when hearing about the practices of people whose faith traditions are different from yours. The Continuum allows you to track your location.

> Where are you on the Continuum in this moment? Where is your school? Your organization? Your classroom or office?

Figure 3.2 describes the characteristics of the environments that might be experienced along the Continuum by a Fish Out of Water and suggests how someone from the dominant culture or a marginalized person might respond.

At the point of *Cultural Destruction*, the dominant culture seeks to eliminate all others, physically or metaphorically. The only codes allowed are those of the dominant culture; the only people in power are in that same group. The goal of the Fish Out of Water is survival. An adult or child in this toxic environment will feel a strong sense of alienation.

Cultural Intolerance is called *Cultural Incapacity* in the original works by Cross (1989) and in the earlier Cultural Proficiency books (Lindsey, Nuri-Robins, Lindsey & Terrell, 2009; Nuri-Robins et al., 2000, 2012). Many of our clients find the concept of *intolerance* easier to understand than *incapacity*. In a Culturally Intolerant environment, differences are demeaned. It is understood that others,

Figure 3.2 The Organizational Climate for Fish Out of Water

	CULTURAL DESTRUCTION	CULTURAL INTOLERANCE	CULTURAL REDUCTION	CULTURAL PRE-COMPETENCE	CULTURAL COMPETENCE	CULTURAL PROFICIENCY
Point on the Continuum	Policies and Practices That EXCLUDE			Policies and Practices That INCLUDE		
Description of the Climate at that Point	The dominant group allows only the cultures of the alphas. Those attempting to use other codes are banished physically or metaphorically. They hide or leave.	The dominant group recognizes that beta groups may use other codes, but those codes are deemed inferior. The beta groups must use the alpha codes to engage with the dominant group.	The dominant group fails to acknowledge that other codes or cultures exist. Those who know more than one set of codes are often closeted. The dominant group, in the spirit of "fairness" and "equality," uses one set of codes—theirs—to communicate with all groups.	The dominant group acknowledges the existence and usefulness of codes used by beta groups. Members of all groups begin to notice when it is appropriate to teach or learn new codes. Efforts to respond appropriately are inconsistent and sometimes ineffective.	Both alpha and beta groups in an environment engage in processes to identify, teach, and learn the cultural codes necessary for effectively interacting with clients, colleagues, and community.	All groups teach and learn the cultural codes of the others. As diverse groups coalesce into new cultures, all use new, universal codes effectively.

42

besides the dominant culture, must be allowed to exist, but life is often difficult for those who are not in power. The beta cultures may know the codes of the dominant groups, but this knowledge is not accompanied with power or access to the privileges of the alphas. Fish Out of Water are purposely disadvantaged by the dominant group at this point on the Continuum. The strategy of the dominant culture in an environment of intolerance is to dominate all other groups. *We cannot kill you, but we can make it very uncomfortable for you to be here.* The result on the Fish Out of Water is extreme marginalization. Their goal is recognition—to be seen as viable and valuable to the environment and to be heard when making contributions or seeking assistance.

The third point on the Continuum as introduced by Cross is *Cultural Blindness*. Color blindness is a familiar term that articulates the goal of well-intentioned people. To be culturally blind is to fail to see differences or to refuse to acknowledge that differences from the dominant culture make a difference. Alphas discount the codes of the Fish Out of Water. Consequently, Fish Out of Water must use only the codes of the alphas and are often forced to deny that they know or use other codes. This results in cultural dualism or closeted behaviors and lifestyles. For young or naïve Fish Out of Water, the result is sometimes dissonance—confusion and discomfort by the conflicting or discordant codes.

We are using the term *Cultural Reduction* instead of *Cultural Blindness* because of pushback we have received from advocates of disabled communities. "There is nothing wrong with being blind," they say. "Don't associate a point of view that you seek to change with something that is a state of being for others that is neither a positive or negative." We are trying out the term *Cultural Reduction*. Let us know what you think. Cultural Reduction is taking the attitude that differences don't make a difference. At this point on the Continuum, people don't see the differences, or they ignore them. The result is they treat everyone the same way—equally—using the same codes—theirs. The goal on the Cultural Proficiency journey is equitable treatment of all, which means diversifying the inputs—that is, giving people what they need, so that the outputs are equal. When people identify with more than one cultural group, if their multicultural identity is not accepted or recognized by the dominant group, the result is dissonance or dualism for the Fish Out of Water.

A person experiences dualism when he must closet aspects of his lifestyle, for example, a gay person passing as straight or a person of color passing as White. When a teacher assumes that everyone in her class speaks English at home, lives with a mother and a father, has access to a personal computer, and can get help with the algebra homework; she has reduced the cultural diversity in the classroom to one group. This limits the approach to teaching and engaging with students in the class and to dissonance among the students who don't fit within the teacher's profile of her class. In this scenario, the teacher does not recognize or use the codes of the students, and to function in this environment, the Fish Out of Water must switch to the codes of the teacher.

When Fish Out of Water have negotiated for acceptance and acknowledgement in their environments, accommodations may be made by the dominant culture. This is *Cultural Pre-Competence*. Well-intentioned actions are taken by the dominant culture, and the results are often superficial, shallow, ineffective, or

> Mrs. Hipkins was teaching her third-grade class about posture. "If you are standing erect, when you stand against the wall your back will be flat," she instructed. The children gathered around a spot in the room where, one at a time, Mrs. Hipkins placed them against the wall. "See how straight he stands." She would praise loudly when the children of European descent backed up to the wall. Then Barbara, the only Black child in the class, had a turn. Her firm round bottom prevented her from aligning her spine to the wall. Mrs. Hipkins put her hand through the arc of light between the base of Barbara's spine and the top of her bottom. "Look children, Barbara has very bad posture; I can't even push her flat to the wall."

inadequate. When a commitment is made to become diverse and inclusive, without collaborating with the newly welcomed groups, members of the dominant culture may use beta codes inappropriately or approach the beta cultures with symbols that are not as significant to the betas as the alphas had expected or, worse, symbols that are offensive to the beta culture. For example, a so-called celebration of diversity at work might be simply a celebration of food and music. *Wear your native costumes* may be offered as an inclusive invitation, but in fact, it is received as an insult because people seeking to be perceived as someone they are not wear costumes. Clothes are worn by people who desire to be seen as themselves. A more appropriate invitation would be, *Wear clothes that reflect your native cultures.*

Cultural Competence is the point on the Continuum where the Essential Elements are employed as standards for practice. At this point, members of the alpha and beta cultures collaborate in processes that assist them to identify, teach, and learn the codes necessary for effectively interacting with clients, colleagues, and community. Fish Out of Water feel affirmed as they engage with those in the dominant culture in the collaborative process of decoding their cultures and code sharing.

The Continuum looks like a line segment with *Cultural Proficiency* as an endpoint. In reality, it is a ray; it signifies a lifetime journey. At this place on the Continuum, all groups code share; they teach and learn the codes of the others. As diverse groups coalesce into new cultures, they use new, universal codes effectively. Resources are distributed equitably, the process of engagement is cocreation, and the result for all in the environment is transformation.

THE BARRIERS TO CULTURAL PROFICIENCY

The Barriers explain why becoming Culturally Proficient is a lifelong journey:

- *Unawareness of the need to adapt*
- *Resistance to change*
- *A sense of entitlement*
- *Institutionalized systems of oppression and privilege*
- *Misuse and abuse of the power that comes with privilege*

The Barriers address both macro-oppressions and micro-oppressions, both of which can be perpetrated systemically and individually. Macro-oppressions, aggressions, and assaults are obviously wrong, because they are violations of the behavioral codes of the dominant culture. Micro-aggressions and assaults are generally directed at individuals who are members of marginalized groups but may be accepted or excused by members of the dominant group, because they are subtle, masked as humor, or perceived as isolated incidents. They are usually comments that reflect a disdain and disregard for people who are different from the dominant group. They are egregious because they are subtle, pervasive, and easily dismissed and denied by the dominant group.

There are strong forces that move people and organizations along the Continuum, away from Culturally Proficient practices. Many people just don't know that they need to change. They are unaware of the need to adapt. Others understand that change is coming but are resistant to change nonetheless. We are often asked by our clients to change everyone in the organization except the leaders who have hired us. "Fix them," they plead, "then everything will be alright."

Keith was the first grandchild on both sides of his family. He was a bright, charming boy in a family that adored its sons. He grew up with the best of everything, from designer baby clothes and studio photographs to admission to Harvard. He had several younger siblings, but their lives were very different from their older brother. They were not mistreated, nor were they denied the many resources afforded to middle-class children. They did not, however, have all the privileges—which included unconditional affection, completed baby books, hundreds of baby pictures, and no hand-me-down clothes—that their older brother had, and while the younger siblings were very aware of the differences, Keith was oblivious.

Whenever he reached a point in his life where he needed something that was not already his, he assumed that he would get it. It never occurred to him that his bounty was acquired only because someone else did not get as much. His sense of entitlement was not malicious, it was shaped by his family culture and informed by his experience. Within organizations, members of the alpha cultures express the same surprise and outrage. Why should they have to give up what was rightfully theirs? Let those who want more, earn what they want. Hence the term *reverse discrimination*. People with a sense of entitlement believe they are being punished as the resources in the environment are redistributed equitably.

Alphas and members of alpha cultures are systemically privileged. They receive the benefits of their alpha status because of nothing they have done and without their permission. That is just the way things are. A blatant example of systemic privilege occurred in a school district we served in the 1980s. There were two junior high schools in the district, and they were across the street from one another. One school served the White children in the district, the other school served the Black and Brown children.

When confronted about the inequity (and illegality) of the system, the board of education members said, "We didn't create the system, it was like that when we got here." True, but once made aware, it was their responsibility to change the system. It is imperative for those on the Cultural Proficiency journey to be aware of systems of privilege and oppression and work to change them.

THE ESSENTIAL ELEMENTS
OF CULTURAL PROFICIENCY .

The Essential Elements answer the question "How do we do it?" Each element is a standard for planning, evaluating, and designing policies, practices, and programs that are Culturally Proficient:

- *Assess Culture.* Assess the cultures that are represented by the organization and the people in the environment.
- *Value Diversity.* Demonstrate an appreciation for the diversity of cultures present. Teach group members when necessary about others who are different from them, and help them to appreciate and understand differences among themselves.
- *Manage the Dynamics of Difference.* Acknowledge historic distrust, release emotional baggage, examine unfounded assumptions, acknowledge personal biases, and understand that good will and an apology do not eliminate the pain of micro-aggressions. Develop tools for effective communication; build skills in problem solving and resolving conflict.
- *Adapt to Diversity.* Change attitudes, perspectives, and practices to acknowledge and welcome all to the environment.
- *Institutionalize Cultural Knowledge.* Develop systems and structures that will outlive the leaders in the organization and will inspire stakeholders to continue the Cultural Proficiency journey.

Code switching or code sharing become Culturally Proficient practices when framed with the Essential Elements.

Assess Culture. Find out who is in the room. What cultures are represented? Whose codes are being used? What are the codes most appropriate for this situation? What codes must be learned and taught by whom?

Value Diversity. Create a climate of mutual appreciation. As the hidden codes are revealed, it is important to share the information as a matter of public discourse. There should be nothing shameful about codes, nor should students be singled out because their codes are different. Sometimes a simple reminder is all that is necessary—for example, "I say 'parents and guardians,' because some children live with a parent, and others live with an adult who is not their parent."

Manage the Dynamics of Difference. Recognize that conflict is natural, and learn to respond to it. Differences in perspectives and approaches are not bad; the tension may be uncomfortable, but it usually is navigable if those in the dominant culture are willing to name the nature of the conflict. "Yes, I know at your other school you were able to go to the restroom without asking, as long as a hall pass was available. Let's talk about why we don't do it here."

Adapt to Diversity. Remember that everyone will have to change something. Embracing a value for diversity and inclusion means being willing to be transformed. Students do the obvious learning, and Culturally Proficient educators, adapting to diversity, learn as well. "OK, then," said Mr. Janc, "When I asked you to bring in a poem that inspires you, I didn't expect the lyrics to a rap song. Go ahead and read or perform it, we'll see what I can learn from your presentation."

Institutionalize Cultural Knowledge. Prepare for a future without your presence. Talk about the codes that represent the various cultures in your environment, not as exceptions to the rules, but as expansions to the rules.

Demonstration that one knows the rules of one's culture is confirmation that this is a group to which one belongs. If you are perceived to belong to a particular group, then it is assumed that you know the unwritten codes. Often, members of the group will say that these things are "common sense," or "everybody knows that . . . " as they gossip or otherwise make judgments about people who are "not abiding by the appropriate codes." When one is in a dominant culture that has expressed a value for diversity and inclusion, it is imperative to teach the codes and to understand the ramifications for not teaching the codes well. A tool that contributes to a Culturally Proficient environment is code switching. In a Culturally Proficient organization, all parties know how to code switch and do so appropriately. Code sharing—teaching your codes and learning the codes of others is a part of the process of cultural transformation.

GOING DEEPER

Reflect

- How do the Guiding Principles inform your work with Fish Out of Water?

Assess

Focus on a particular environment and assess how well code switching is supported.

Assess Culture

Find out who is in the room.

1. What is the nature of diversity in the environment?
2. How is it changing?
3. What codes are being used?

4. What cultures are present in the alpha and beta groups?

5. Who knows whose codes?

Value Diversity

Create a climate of mutual appreciation.

6. What language is used to describe the various groups?

7. Are attempts made to approach each group equitably?

8. Is an atmosphere sustained that allows the members of the group to teach and learn about one another?

9. What is the process for inducting new groups into the culture?

Manage the Dynamics of Difference

Recognize that conflict is natural and learn to respond to it.

10. What natural conflicts are likely to occur?

11. What skills are needed to manage the conflicts?

12. How do you recognize conflicts within and between groups?

13. What communication issues may occur because of historical distrust relationships?

Adapt to Diversity

Remember that everyone will have to change something.

14. How has the alpha culture changed to accommodate the betas?

15. Have change opportunities been assessed and addressed?

16. What processes are created to induct the betas into the alpha culture?

17. What have you done to promote code sharing?

Institutionalize Cultural Knowledge

Prepare for a future without your presence.

18. What ongoing practices have been introduced?

19. How will the stakeholders ensure that what they have learned will be shared with others?

20. What structures have been put in place so that good work will continue and the people and the organization will keep learning?

Discuss

- Tell a story about when you experienced unearned privilege.
- Using the Continuum of Cultural Proficiency, discuss the health of your organizational pond.
- How far do the Fish in your pond have to swim to get to the Cultural Proficiency end of the Continuum?

4

How Fish Out of Water Are Marginalized

In every organization, there are systems of oppression and systems of privilege that push people who do not meet or use the norms of the dominant culture to the margins of the group. These systems are usually subtle and are often explained away as inconsequential, because they are the product of unconscious biases.

F ish Out of Water are often new or different. They may be new to the system or approach the work in that system differently than most others. Fish Out of Water may be passionate nuisances, truth tellers, exotics, or visionaries. While often invisible, they see what others don't see or see what others dismiss as unimportant or inoffensive. They are people who might not fit into the mainstream; they are viewed as add-ons to the group or uninvited guests rather than community members. Fish Out of Water are people who do not or cannot use the cultural codes of their environments and consequently are minimized, targeted, and marginalized by members of the dominant group.

Even when Fish Out of Water can code switch, they may be excluded because some codes cannot be masked, switched, or changed. These are groups based on race or ethnicity, language, gender, age, ability, and other categories that cannot be changed. Other Fish are excluded because they do not know the codes that are being used, or they do not use the codes appropriately. They may look like the members of the group that make the rules, but for other reasons, they are different from them. Sociological terms for feeling out of place or being excluded from a group include *alienation, marginalization, dissonance, dualism,* and *negotiation for acceptance.*

THE DOMINANT CULTURE

Some people are uncomfortable with the term *dominant* group, particularly when they do not feel dominant or powerful. If you never have to think about the groups you are in, if cultural identity is not made an issue for you by others, if you rarely think about fitting in, you are an insider and you are probably a member of the dominant group. That means you have privileges you may not be aware of—privileges that you didn't earn and probably didn't ask for just because you are a member of that group. These privileges include acceptance by and access to those in power and the benefit of the doubt that you are indeed where you belong.

In a diverse environment, there are alpha groups and beta groups. There is great comfort and acceptance of using the terms *alpha* and *beta* to refer to members of the animal kingdom; while they may be used less frequently when referring to people, the power differential in relationships exists nonetheless. The alpha group sets the norms for interactions and often names the beta groups. Alphas are *people* or *normal;* betas are *others.* People who are in an alpha group are often unaware of the advantages they have because the cultural rules benefit them, consequently their micro-advantages are sometimes hard for them to discern and easy to deny. Another term for alpha group is *dominant* or *mainstream culture.*

Every group comes with certain privileges or entitlements. However, alpha groups or dominant groups have the power to name, marginalize, and oppress others. This oppression may be physically violent and overt, or it may be subtle, pervasive, and insidious—hard to identify unless you are being targeted. Although you may not feel like an alpha, you may belong to an alpha group. You may be the alpha in your family or social group. Your occupation, social group, or organization may be an alpha organization. Some people belong to many alpha groups. In the United States the alpha groups with the most social power include people of North Western European descent, people whose sexuality is perceived as straight, and men. Fish Out of Water may belong to alpha groups, but because of how they are in the world, they are still marginalized and consequently betas. All betas are not necessarily Fish Out of Water.

> Do you belong to any alpha groups? In what groups are you an alpha? Who are the alphas in your organization?

TARGETS AND AGENTS

One way of looking at dominant cultures and how they contribute to the marginalization of Fish Out of Water is by understanding the concept of targets and agents. Simply put, agents are the perpetrators, and targets are the victims, based upon the groups to which they belong. A target group is the non-dominant group when looking at categories such as race, ethnicity, gender, sexual orientation, and socioeconomic status. One's status as an alpha or a beta may change with the social setting, but target or agent status rarely changes. An agent group is always a power-up group. A target group is always power down.

A target group is the object of both micro-aggressions—that is, ridicule and demeaning stereotype—and macro-aggressions, blatant and overt discrimination. A target is the person who gets picked on, laughed at, or bullied or ignored because of his or her membership in a particular group. People in target groups may sometimes perceive individual members of agent groups as prejudiced or biased when they are not. People in agent groups often assume people in target groups are all exactly like the negative stereotypes held about the target people.

An individual who is targeted can be in a target group or be a low-status member of an alpha group. You can be an alpha in a target group or a beta in an agent group. Because alpha and beta status is flexible, this is situational power. Target and agent status, however, does not change; this is institutional and systemic power. Fish Out of Water are marginalized because of their target status, because they are betas in the dominant culture, and because those in the dominant culture are unaware of the many daily micro-assaults to which the Fish Out of Water are subjected.

Agents are the groups with the most societal power. Agents pick on, objectify, and oppress—overtly or through micro-assaults—people who are members of target groups. You can be a member of an agent group and not behave as an agent, but you may be perceived as an agent. While you may not be responsible for the perceptions of others, you are responsible for being sensitive to how your actions may unintentionally be hurtful to others. You are also responsible for monitoring any unconscious bias you may have toward target groups.

> Do you feel like a target in any of the groups to which you belong? Are you perceived as an agent in any of your groups? How do the people you serve get targeted?

MICRO-AGGRESSIONS

In any setting, you may witness practices or behaviors that by themselves may be slightly questionable or not even noticed but are experienced as micro-aggressions, micro-assaults, or micro-inequities by the targets (Sue, 2010a). These practices are wrong, but often, when the target complains, their protests are dismissed as inconsequential or the targets are judged as overly sensitive. Comments that imply that a minority person only got their job because of affirmative action or that a woman is over emotional or that poor people are stupid are micro-aggressions. Raising an eyebrow and saying, "More?" to an overweight person eating a second helping is a micro-aggression. Telling someone who has just come out to you, "Oh, you don't look gay," is a micro-aggression.

> The teachers at an elementary school that was changing from predominately White to predominately non-White were implementing an anti-bullying campaign. The plan included a week of activities called "Moving from Darkness to Light." On the first day, all of the teachers wore black. "This is Dark Day," they said. "Bullying is bad; bad things are dark. We wear black to remind children that we don't want them to be dark." Their plan was for everyone to wear white clothing on the last day of the campaign. The anti-bullying program the teachers had developed was wonderful. The teachers did not, however, foresee how their language might affect the children of color in their classrooms. "All dark things are bad?" one child asked, as he looked pointedly at his Mixteco classmate. "Yes," the teacher said emphatically.

Macro-aggressions are obviously wrong and offensive behaviors or policies. Micro-aggressions are often treated as isolated incidents, jokes, or insensitive remarks that should be forgiven and forgotten. Micro-aggressors may not even know they have done something wrong, because their bias is unconscious or an implicit part of the culture. Because they are often overlooked and usually repeated over time, micro-aggressions are pervasive and egregious. Unconscious or implicit bias and stereotyping are dynamics that confound every interaction because they are complex, difficult to discern, and easy to deny (Banaji & Greenwald, 2013; Dweck, Chiu, & Hong, 1995).

> Can you think of examples of language or behaviors that may be perceived by the targets in your group as macro-aggressions or micro-assaults? What can you do to make it safer for targeted or marginalized people?

The Barriers to Cultural Proficiency are major factors in the exclusionary practices that push Fish Out of Water to the margins of their environments. Unawareness of the need to remedy a situation or failure to do so even when the need is apparent are preeminent Barriers. Unawareness is connected to implicit and unconscious bias. Resistance to change often occurs because the alphas in the environment do not understand or recognize how their individual and collective privilege silences or marginalizes Fish Out of Water. In *Dual Pathways to a Better America* (2012), members of the American Psychological Association discuss the impact of exclusion in relationship to systemic structures as well as on the individual. Argyris and Schon (1974) describe how one can take an inappropriate action based upon implicit bias and overreliance on stereotypes by climbing the ladder of inference. CampbellJones, CampbellJones, and Lindsey (2010, p. 34–38) provide an excellent description of the ladder of inference and Argyris' double-loop learning.

Early and continuous marginalization is a major reason for students dropping out or being pushed out of schools. Data on achievement and discipline disparities according to cultural, racial, or gender differences continue to challenge schools and suggest that many students are being underserved or mis-served. The Office of Civil Rights reports major disparities in the application of exclusionary practices, including suspensions, restraint, and seclusion, on the basis of race, ethnicity, gender, and disability (2014). While people are told that all children can learn and bullying is wrong and this is no place for hate, there are people in the environment who remain unseen and voiceless—or worse—targeted and under-served because their needs are not being met. These are the people who have not figured out the hidden curriculum, the unwritten rules—the codes—of the organization, or who, for a variety of reasons, don't fit in. People are served in varying degrees by the dominant culture, and when there is no code sharing, when members of non-dominant groups do not know the codes or have not learned to code switch, they cannot participate fully or derive all of the benefits from being in a group.

The structural changes from preschool and kindergarten to first grade can be confusing for many children. After the rather open and interactive learning opportunities provided for preK and kindergarten children, first graders are expected to behave in a more controlled manner by sitting at a desk and conforming to a new set of norms, including whole group work. These are norms that are usually at odds with learned home behaviors as well. These changes affect boys of color in ways that often impact their future experiences at school. When expectations are differentially applied by teachers, based on unconscious biases and stereotypes, marginalization and feelings of alienation are common results.

The effects of implicit bias on students are myriad, from psychological to physical (Kirwan Institute for the Study of Race and Ethnicity, 2014). Reduction in levels of trust, self-esteem, and physical well-being can lead to even more limiting behaviors, such as depression, abuse of self and others, and even suicide. To survive, students develop a range of coping skills, from masking themselves to fighting back. Which of these responses are used depends largely on what has been learned at home or perceived as most effective at the time. These responses can take the form of survival tactics where Fish Out of Water buffer themselves from hostilities or mask their real selves in order to be accepted.

Baysu describes dualism as a two-edged sword, often resulting in discrimination in both cultures. For multiracial children, marginalization is intensified when their dual identities make them a minority in two cultures (Boykin & Toms, 1985). A gay child may be criticized by his gender nonconforming friends for not being out, while the straight children tease and bully him because they suspect he is gay. The rules of engagement are very complex, often contradictory, and consequently confusing, particularly for children.

When children or adults have not learned the rules—the hidden curriculum—of their school or workplace, they are marginalized and often feel like Fish Out of Water. To assure the success of children and their families, leaders must discern and teach the cultural expectations of the school environment. They must also teach students how to do this as a lifelong practice, to learn any new environment. Sometimes, however, people are marginalized because they are different from the majority, and regardless of how many codes they learn, they will never be accepted into the dominant culture. They will always be targets until the dominant culture changes.

Figure 4.1 presents sociological terms that describe the various ways people can be excluded. This chart can be used as a tool for sharing personal stories and for assessing the environment you are working in. As you look

> Miracle Bridge Park was created in a green space between a wealthy White neighborhood surrounding a major university, and a poor Black and Brown neighborhood on its margins. The park was designed to be accessible by all children regardless of physical limitations. Rabiah lived on the poorer, south side of the park and was pleased to take her six-year-old granddaughter, Ayan, to play. At the park, Ayan approached an older, White girl and asked to play with her. The White child said, "I can't play with you because you're Black. If I play with you, and breathe the same air, I will die in two hours." Hurt and embarrassed, Ayan returned to her grandmother.

Figure 4.1	How People Get Pushed to the Margins

Social Experience	Your Experience	Emotional Content	Situations at Work
Alienation Out of place. Not fitting in. Not belonging to any group. *Example:*			
Marginalization Identifying with two groups but not fitting in either. Being rejected by both groups and relegated to the margins. *Example:*			
Dissonance Discordant. Disharmony. Feeling out of synch, offbeat, out of tune with your surroundings. *Example:*			
Dualism Being involved in two cultures and having to hide that fact from one of the cultural groups. *Example:*			
Negotiation for Acceptance Having to prove that one deserves to be in a particular role or environment. *Example:*			
Affirmation Belonging to two or more cultural groups, with both groups knowing and appreciating that you are part of the other. *Example:*			
Transformation People from different cultures interacting with one another over time. All are changed for the better because of the experience. *Example:*			

at this list, think about the ponds you have been in and your stories about them. The stories you choose to tell will be correlated to how important fitting in was for you in a particular situation. Some people really want to fit in. Some people don't fit in and don't care. Other people know they don't fit, but they can't walk away for any number of good reasons; that is usually where the pain and anger of being marginalized start.

How People Get Pushed to the Margins

Here are stories Fish Out of Water might experience as they move along the Continuum.

Elimination

- Alonzo is a large, very sociable African American second grader. He responds loudly to one of his White classmates, who complained tearfully to the teacher. The teacher thinks Alonzo is out of control and orders him out of the classroom. Alonzo demands to know why he can't stay in class and refuses to leave. The teacher calls security, who removes Alonzo from the class and begins the suspension process. This is the first of a series of school suspensions for Alonzo before he drops out in seventh grade.

- Elizabeth was hired by Maggie to be her assistant dean. Maggie assumed her responsibilities a month before the university president asked Elizabeth to resign. The faculty in this small, suburban School of Allied Health Professions was a closed club of academics who were not quite good enough for major universities. They affirmed their own false sense of competence by bullying anyone who attempted to raise their standards. They had blocked every initiative that Maggie sought to implement as dean and were celebrating her departure when Elizabeth assumed her position. "Well, we got rid of the dean, they boasted, we will get rid of her flunky too." Maggie, affirmed to her coach that she could work with anyone, a week before she too, was fired.

Alienation

- Vanessa was a new kid. In an attempt to make her feel welcome and comfortable, her teacher introduced Vanessa to her classmates by saying, "Because Vanessa is a foster child, she will need some extra support from you all in getting to know the school and neighborhood." Needless to say, rather than feeling helped Vanessa was crushed. The teacher had used the "F" word (foster child), a connotation that she was unwanted and uncared for. The kids teased her, the teachers patronized her. She was afraid to discuss her school problems at home because it could lead to another relocation—always a scary situation. She was unwilling to talk to her teachers because she feared further humiliation.

- Mary was in her mid-forties when she married a navy physician. They lived in her hometown, where she got along well with their neighbors and his civilian friends. Things changed when they moved to a new city and resided in military housing on the base. "I would have been more comfortable on Mars," Mary confided to a friend. "There are rules for everything. They treat me like I am in the navy too. No one seems to understand that the navy rules aren't mine."

Marginalization

- Beverly is the only child of a former college athlete. She is a good soccer player and wears jeans and sneakers most of the time. Because she prefers to play sports whenever she can, she is around boys more than girls. She cannot, however, hang out with them in the locker room, and they do not include her in the socializing after the games. Beverly has no girl-friends either; the girls she knows tease her in person and taunt her on Facebook.

- As a consultant, Larry understands the organization and helps the people who work there, but he is not one of them. They like him well enough, but they know he doesn't really belong, so he is treated well but kept at a distance. He never gets invited to the after-work gatherings or the celebrations they share that help to make them a community.

- Stacy and Allen left their home in Southern California so Stacy could take a job at a university in Alabama. Stacy was immediately caught up in the activities of the academic community. She had classes to plan and teach, other professors to meet, and committee meetings to attend. Her husband took on the role of primary caregiver for their young son, something a number of his friends did in California. In this new environment, Allen had trouble finding peers. Most of the men worked, and their leisure activities did not include chess, old movies, or gaming, all of which Allen loved.

Dualism

- Noel is fairly new to Eastside Middle School. He is an accomplished singer and is always asked to perform in school performances, which he does occasionally. He is a member of a local gang, because he believes membership in it is necessary for his survival in his neighborhood. His friends in the gang are not impressed with his school activities, so he hides his involvement from the gang or declines to participate in school activities that he might enjoy. Noel is also very careful not to share his gang involvement with members of the school choir or teachers.

- Kathryn runs the business started by her father. She networks at the businessmen's meetings that are part of this male-dominated industry, where the men are cordial to her because of the relationship they had with her father. After a few years of proving she knew what she was doing, they began to accept her and include her in the golf tournaments and other events where deals were made. Kathryn's new colleagues thought she was as conservative as she dressed. The only differences they could cite were Kathryn's age and gender. They had no idea that her politics were very progressive and her friends included gay men, lesbians, and people of color.

Dissonance

- Suzanne had blossomed at the Montessori school she attended since she was three. Then when she was in the fifth grade, her family moved. Suzanne and her parents were confident that she would do well in the new suburban public school, because she loved school and had done so well up to that time. Now, she just can't figure it out. Her teacher tells her what subject to study, what book to use, and what pages she is sup-posed to read. "Keep up with the rest of the class," the teacher says. "How can I explore and discover if I have to do what everyone else does?" Suzanne laments.

- Jacob is a third-year teacher, new to school in the inner city, where most of the students are low-income Hispanic and African American. He teaches an advanced placement history course, in which the majority of the students are poor readers and have almost no writing skills. Jacob asks the principal if there has been a mistake in the class assignment; he is astounded when the principal tells him, "You will have to adjust your understanding of what advanced placement means with those kids."

Negotiation for Acceptance

- Taylor just moved with his family from an urban neighborhood to an exclusive, gated community. At his new school, he enrolled in advanced placement courses, which he had been in at his previous school. Despite his attempts to join study groups, he never felt welcomed; everyone, even the teachers, treated him like an interloper. It was only when he earned the school's highest score on a national standardized test that his teachers began to include him as an active member of the class. It took longer for classmates to accept him.

- Bill's fiancée, Analiese, had been homeschooled and then apprenticed with a jeweler in her early twenties. She was well read but unlettered, and her future mother-in-law was not impressed. "Good marriages occur when the couple is evenly yoked," Bill's mother said. "That girl doesn't have your education or experiences. She won't be able to carry on a conversation with your friends or their wives. She will never fit in with our family."

Figure 4.2 correlates these terms to the points on the Cultural Proficiency Continuum describing the type of marginalization that Fish Out of Water experience at each point along the Continuum. The left side of the Cultural Proficiency Continuum describes policies, practices, and behaviors that exclude or marginalize people and create Fish Out of Water. The extent to which people feel excluded or marginalized is affected by the degree to which codes are taught and shared, the level of cultural conflict present in the system, and the ability of group members to change policies and practices. Disaffection can have significant negative consequences on the individual and the group, promoting antisocial responses, self and other abusive behaviors, and

Using one or more of these terms, tell of a time when you felt like a Fish Out of Water. You may use Figure 4.1 to guide your discussion:

- **Alienation**—You feel disconnected from the group, with no entry point for making a difference. People are playing by rules they haven't shared with you.
- **Marginalization**—You are not engaging with the people in the environment who are influential or have formal power. You are not in the mainstream.
- **Dualism**—You belong to two groups, but neither may know you are part of the other. Because one of your groups is not tolerated, you are in the closet.
- **Dissonance**—You are mentally and emotionally prepared for one thing, which does not happen. Little in the environment meets your expectations.
- **Negotiating for Acceptance**—You have to justify your presence in the group because people assume you are not qualified to be there.

mutual mistrust. This chapter has focused on the left side and center of the Continuum; the right side is included in Figure 4.2 so that you can contrast the effect of a healthy climate on Fish Out of Water.

Affirmation and Transformation

At the far right end of the Continuum, the points describe how people are embraced and included. Affirmation and transformation are not ways that people get marginalized; they are ways that people are included. It is here that code switching between groups is normalized, and code sharing becomes the norm.

Multicultural affirmation occurs when you are part of two or more cultures or communities, everyone knows that about you, and they think it is a good thing. Multicultural transformation is what happens when people have experiences that enable them to learn about their similarities and

Figure 4.2 Effects of the Environment on Fish Out of Water

		CULTURAL DESTRUCTION	CULTURAL INTOLERANCE	CULTURAL REDUCTION	CULTURAL PRE-COMPETENCE	CULTURAL COMPETENCE	CULTURAL PROFICIENCY
	Point on the Continuum	*Policies and Practices That EXCLUDE*			*Policies and Practices That INCLUDE*		
Ch 4	***Effect on Fish Out of Water***	Alienation Elimination	Marginalization	Dualism Dissonance	Negotiation	Affirmation	Transformation
		Surviving		Maintaining		Thriving	
Ch 3	***Description of the Climate at that Point***	The dominant group allows only the cultures of the alphas. Those attempting to use other codes are banished physically or metaphorically. They hide or leave.	The dominant group recognizes that beta groups may use other codes, but those codes are deemed inferior. The beta groups must use the alpha codes to engage with the dominant group.	The dominant group fails to acknowledge that other codes or cultures exist. Those who know more than one set of codes are often closeted. The dominant group, in the spirit of "fairness" and "equality," uses one set of codes—theirs—to communicate with all groups.	The dominant group acknowledges the existence and usefulness of codes used by beta groups. Members of all groups begin to notice when it is appropriate to teach or learn new codes. Efforts to respond appropriately are inconsistent and sometimes ineffective.	Both alpha and beta groups in an environment engage in processes to identify, teach, and learn the cultural codes necessary for effectively interacting with clients, colleagues, and community.	All groups teach and learn the cultural codes of the others. As diverse groups coalesce into new cultures, all use new, universal codes effectively.

differences and they grow and are changed in the process. It is those experiences when you feel connected to everyone present and changed forever.

Everybody wants to belong. Leiberman (2013) suggests that Maslow got it wrong. It is not food, clothing, and shelter that people need most, it is belonging. If a child belongs to no one, she will not get the basics of life that will sustain her. As she grows and matures, the need for one caretaker expands in concentric circles to family and community. It is from this first caretaker and in these primary groups that she learns her first codes—her human nature. It is consequently human nature to want to be around others who affirm one's values and styles of interaction. When she sees her values and behavioral styles mirrored by others, she is affirmed. People are excluded or pushed to the margins when they do not affirm, by mirroring, the people around them. When they do not look like the cultural group in which they are interacting, or the style with which they engage does not meet the cultural expectations of the dominant group, they may be pushed to the edges—or out.

GOING DEEPER

Reflect

- How do you recognize Fish Out of Water?
- What internal indicators do you have that let you know something is not right?

Assess

Who Are the Fish Out of Water?
Using Figure 4.1, answer the following questions:

1. How does your organization or group create Fish Out of Water?

2. What names are used to describe the various groups of outsiders?

3. What do you think might be the toughest situations for these people?

4. How might you help Fish Out of Water in the various situations you have described?

Discuss

- What can you do to make it safer and less oppressive for people who are not a part of the dominant culture?

5

The Consequences of Fitting In

Fish Out of Water may choose to stay in toxic or otherwise unwelcoming environments for many reasons. If they stay, the cost to them personally and the benefits they derive from the environment will range, depending on how they decide to engage.

THE BENEFITS OF FITTING IN

Robbins (2011) and Gladwell (2011) suggest that there is much to be learned from and admired by those who don't always fit. They suggest that in some ways, creating conditions for outsiders to grow and maintain their outlier status can produce very positive results and advancements in the long run. This is rarely the case in most situations. Generally, Fish Out of Water find themselves perplexed, resentful, and victimized. Most of the time, the principle of Cultural Proficiency is evident: Members of non-dominant cultures have to be at least bicultural. The onus of adapting falls to the betas in the group. Consequently, fitting into a culture does not always come easily or without cost.

People who don't fit in may stay in an environment that is not right for them, because the results of leaving would create even worse circumstances. The major benefit of fitting in for the Fish Out of Water is access to power and resources that are found at the center. Code switching, like second language learning, opens the door to new worlds and more options. Code switching gives one greater access to information and people who are a part of the dominant group. First it is a tool that adds to the individual's repertoire of social skills. Making polite conversation with strangers, offering and asking for help, and using the correct fork at the table are all skills of varying levels of importance. Knowing what is important and being able to use the appropriate currency of social exchange are skills that are highly valued in almost all groups.

Children must be taught to code switch between the language of the home and the language of the school, for the appropriate time, place, audience, and communicative purpose so they are explicitly aware of how to select the appropriate language to use in the given context (Wheeler & Swords, 2004, p. 14). Without the use of appropriate social codes, Fish Out of Water are teased, bullied, shunned, and excluded from community events. Adults are not considered for promotions; children are labeled and dismissed as below average, not college material, at-risk, low achievers. Even the quiet, reserved introvert may be perceived as snobbish, with members of the dominant groups saying, "She never speaks to anyone; she thinks she is better than us."

Fitting in is not necessarily giving in to the new culture. Nor is it adapting all of the cultural norms and mores of a second culture to the exclusion of the first. That is assimilation. Code switching is the agile and conscious movement between two or more cultures. It is a social lubricant, like using two languages fluently. In the best of circumstances, everyone code shares. Members of the dominant culture as well as the non-dominant culture use the codes of the other. While the benefits of code switching are many, the costs of fitting in might include the stress of code switching or the possibility that the person trying to fit in may lose himself in the process. Prolonged mask wearing is uncomfortable, and it denies those in the environment from taking full advantage of all the diversity that is there.

CODE SWITCHING HAS ITS LIMITATIONS

Code switching may decrease the occurrences of targeted micro-aggressions for some Fish Out of Water. Code switching, however, cannot make people of color White; nor will code switching cause the lame to walk, the dumb to talk, or the blind to see. Code switching will definitely not open the door for women to join the old boys' clubs (Nuri-Robins & Terrell, 1987). It is not a panacea; it is an additional tool necessary in a multicultural society and is most effectively used by members of both dominant and non-dominant groups—when members of each group code share—learning some of the codes of the other groups.

Many Fish Out of Water choose not to take this route; they walk to the margins, instead of being pushed, and stay there. People who are different become catalysts for change. On the margins are many who don't fit into the dominant culture of organizations: Truth Tellers, Exotics, Crazies, Visionaries, and Paradigm Shifters. There is protection on the margins because the Fish Out of Water can swim with their own kind; being part of a group and not alone gives them additional power. While most people who are too different from the dominant group are excluded by those groups, they are often given leeway that those in the center do not have. They are not pressed to move outside of their comfort zones. Less is expected of the excluded, so there is space to do more of what they want to do—within certain boundaries—they are free to be assertively individualistic.

PATRICK'S STORY

Patrick, a high school sophomore, is from a low-income, Southern, African American background where his parents valued but had not received a good education. His parents trust the schools completely to provide a fair, transformative experience for Patrick. While they have experienced racism all of their lives, Patrick's parents believe that schools are the only pathway to success and that issues of race should be dealt with at home and tolerated at school. Patrick, on the other hand, knows that he is stereotyped and limited because of his race. He is prepared to resist all that is school and does this by refusing to comply with the dress codes, refusing to use standard English (which he speaks fluently) in the classroom, and refusing to exert the effort to earn more than a passing grade in his classes.

As adults, Fish Out of Water may choose to stay in an unwelcoming environment for financial or career reasons. Juvenile Fish Out of Water often have to stay where they are because the environment that marginalizes them is school or home, but some negotiate their leaving through parents and counselors. Others, by acting out, may orchestrate their departures only to be further excluded as foster children or targets of the juvenile justice system. If they choose to stay, Fish Out of Water can code switch or stay on the margins. If they stay on the margins, then they must learn to survive as a loner or join the community of outsiders.

The outsider communities in schools have names like emo, geek, skater, and indie. Geography, generation, and the particular school culture adds other labels to the list. Adult outsiders also have names: strange, nutcase, nerd, airhead, nonconformist, drama queen, and not a team player are some of the more common ones. Each of these outsider groups has norms, that is, codes, and it is possible to be ejected from an outsider group for not conforming to a particular group of nonconformists. It is most unfortunate for an outsider to be rejected by sister outcasts.

What are some of the names of the outsider groups at your school or place of work? Do you know any of them? Are you a member of any of them?

Wearing a Mask

It is not, however, uncommon for an outsider, a Fish Out of Water, to choose to be alone rather than to publically associate with other outsiders. It is this internalized disdain for the outcasts that sometimes drives the Fish Out of Water back into the pond. To survive in these unfriendly waters, the marginalized Fish have to camouflage themselves, blending into the environment until they look like dappled sunlight on the leaves of plants or like the other Fish who are comfortable and, perhaps, unconscious of the privilege of swimming safely in the middle of the pond.

This camouflage is called wearing a mask (Dunbar, 1896). The metaphorical mask is worn to camouflage real feelings and responses to the world. Wearing a mask may be a conscious choice to gain acceptance, to be left alone, to keep one's job, or to stop bullies from their attacks by using cultural codes that are appropriate for a particular environment. When one wears a mask for so long that he never steps from behind it or he perceives his authentic self to be the one presented by the mask, he has become assimilated. He has merged with the dominant culture and no longer abides by the norms or behaviors of his first or native cultures. Some, especially those in the dominant culture, might say he has adapted well. These Fish Out of

Water, for example, may appear, to the dominant group, to have adapted well:

- A Guatemalan child who speaks flawless English but no longer speaks Spanish to his grandmother.
- A bullied child who joins the chorus of supporting sycophants, while the alpha bully continues to terrorize the schoolyard.
- A small-framed, unattractive artist who excels in English classes, does passably in math and science, but secretly longs for the art and music he has not pursued because he fears he is not good enough.
- An introverted manager who prefers evenings alone listening to classical music now regularly joins her colleagues at the local tavern. She has traded her books for a glass of sparkling water with lime, which she nurses like a gin and tonic.

These people may have adapted well, but they have lost themselves in the process. Code switching initially may have enhanced their acceptability, but not switching back has caused them to lose their identities so much that they no longer engage effectively in their native or most desired environments. In these examples, they are no longer switching. They have crossed over and stayed in the second culture; they have adopted the new cultural norms. If this is their goal, we salute them; it is our experience, however, that this is not a goal as much as it is a plight. Code switching as a tactic or skill that allows one to function in two or more cultures does not imply that one subjugates his native culture to a dominant one; rather, it means one understands the rules of both and uses both codes effectively.

Healthy, inclusive organizational cultures require mindful management by leaders who value diversity, have skills for bringing people together, and encourage code sharing. Unhealthy organizational or classroom cultures exclude and marginalize many groups of people. There are times when a toxic culture is also strong, with unified values and purpose (think Nazi Germany). In such a homogeneous culture, creative conflicts are uninvited and challenges to the status quo are unacceptable. Generally, hostile, toxic environments tend to be unpleasant and stress producing for almost everyone in them. This results in high turnover, absenteeism, and low morale; both internal and external customer service is poor. When group members are rendered invisible or voiceless, the organization cannot benefit from the harmony of diverse voices.

Inequitable distribution of resources and power produces resentful employees who seek to take what they can from the organization without serving the organization's clients or communities. If the employee is uncomfortable in a hostile environment, he will be focused on survival and retaliation, not on service to his clients. This results in lower productivity, lower service statistics in an organization, lower achievement scores in a school, and ultimately lawsuits against the Culturally Destructive policies and practices.

WHEN NO MASK WILL FIT

Many young people feel that individual expression is more important than fitting in. The right to assert one's individuality and idiosyncratic authenticity must be respected. Others do not understand the value of being a member of a group. "What difference does it make what I wear?" they say, "I'm just here to do a job." The difference is that outsiders are preyed upon, targeted, and often destroyed spiritually or physically. There are some people who can thrive in this kind of environment. They assert their right to live authentically and are willing to suffer the consequences for being themselves without wearing a mask at any time. This does not mean they never code switch. Most people who interact with others code switch—intimate to formal, peer to superior, insider to outsider—people on the autism spectrum are obvious exceptions. Everyone, however, does not code switch appropriately from one cultural milieu to another. This type of code switching is a choice and may make the difference between surviving a toxic environment, functioning moderately well, or thriving in it.

Throughout his adolescence, for Eric, a gay, White man, code switching meant attempting to embody more traditional masculine stereotypes as a means of survival. "I was clearly unsuccessful at this endeavor, considering the number of times that I was harassed by my peers," he told us. There are still times in his life that he feels that he must pass "or at least assume a disguise," in order to preserve his sense of safety. But, he admonishes, there are some instances in which code switching means suppressing one's true nature, and the consequences are chronic unhappiness, addiction, and even suicide. In such instances, it is the responsibility of organizations and larger society to adapt to the differences of the marginalized. Code switching can serve as an adaptive mechanism or survival skill in a world of injustice and oppression. At the same time, the privileged and powerful have a moral responsibility to critically examine and disturb circumstances that place so many people on the margins of society.

While fitting in is not important to some outsiders, some marginalized groups cannot ever fit in. Switching codes will not make a person of color White or a gay person straight, an abstract thinker concrete or a transgender or intersexed person cisgender. It is important to develop the value for diversity among the members of the dominant group and to nurture an environment in which the alphas do not target the outsiders with micro-aggressions that result from their Cultural Reductionism or Cultural Pre-Competence. At the same time, it is important for those who manage and mentor the marginalized to distinguish between those who need help and want it and those who want to be left alone. The cost to the organization of not having a variety of cultural codes represented is the many missed opportunities for learning and growing when a large percentage of the population remains on the margins.

SURVIVE, THRIVE, OR MAINTAIN?

In Figure 5.1, another row has been added to the Fish Out of Water Continuum. To review, the bottom row shows the points along the Continuum moving from Cultural Destruction to Cultural Proficiency. The three columns on the left side of the Continuum reflect organizational environments and individual practices that marginalize and exclude those who are not part of the dominant culture. The three columns on the right side of the Continuum reflect polices and practices, both individual and institutional, that include the beta groups. This means that both the alphas and the betas are learning from and growing with each other. When examining code switching on the left side, only the betas are code switching. On the right side, code sharing is taking place among all groups.

In Chapter 4, we discussed how Fish Out of Water are marginalized. The various types of marginalization are summarized in the row added for that chapter, the effect of the different environments on the Fish Out of Water. In this chapter, we have highlighted the consequences of fitting in. Code sharing adds to the richness and health of the environment, but every Fish Out of Water does not have code sharing as a goal. Because the costs and benefits of fitting in vary from one person to another, the efforts they make to code switch will also vary. If the person doesn't want much from the environment, his goals may be simply to survive or be tolerated. Patrick, the high school sophomore introduced in this chapter, is not interested in sharing his codes or using the codes of the dominant culture. His goal at school is to survive what he experiences as a hostile environment and to have the dominant culture merely tolerate his presence. He will survive physically, but with his attitude and without an advocate, he will have to struggle to earn passing grades.

The Guatemalan child who has learned English so well that he can no longer speak Spanish to his grandmother will

Figure 5.1 The Process of Fitting In

		CULTURAL DESTRUCTION	CULTURAL INTOLERANCE	CULTURAL REDUCTION	CULTURAL PRE-COMPETENCE	CULTURAL COMPETENCE	CULTURAL PROFICIENCY
	Point on the Continuum	*Policies and Practices That EXCLUDE*			*Policies and Practices That INCLUDE*		
Ch 5	**Goals for Fish Out of Water**	Survival	Tolerance	Recognition	Inclusion	Engagement	Equity
	Response of the Fish Out of Water	Buffering	Masking	Code switching	Bridging	Code sharing	Bonding
Ch 4	**Effect on Fish Out of Water**	Alienation Elimination	Marginalization	Dualism Dissonance	Negotiation	Affirmation	Transformation
		Surviving		Maintaining		Thriving	
Ch 3	**Description of the Climate at that Point**	The dominant group allows only the cultures of the alphas. Those attempting to use other codes are banished physically or metaphorically. They hide or leave.	The dominant group recognizes that beta groups may use other codes, but those codes are deemed inferior. The beta groups must use the alpha codes to engage with the dominant group.	The dominant group fails to acknowledge that other codes or cultures exist. Those who know more than one set of codes are often closeted. The dominant group, in the spirit of "fairness" and "equality," uses one set of codes—theirs—to communicate with all groups.	The dominant group acknowledges the existence and usefulness of codes used by beta groups. Members of all groups begin to notice when it is appropriate to teach or learn new codes. Efforts to respond appropriately are inconsistent and sometimes ineffective.	Both alpha and beta groups in an environment engage in processes to identify, teach, and learn the cultural codes necessary for effectively interacting with clients, colleagues, and community.	All groups teach and learn the cultural codes of the others. As diverse groups coalesce into new cultures, all use new, universal codes effectively.

also survive in the dominant culture, but he may become an outsider in his native environment. The introverted manager has found a way to be recognized and included in her work environment, but she has given up aspects of her life that are important to her. Her professional existence is dualistic; her colleagues know little about who she really is and what kind of social activities she prefers. The colleagues of many introverts who have learned the codes of extroversion are surprised to hear close friends of their coworker described as quiet or shy or introspective. Introverts work hard to fit into their extroverted worlds and sometimes suffer from the stress of their environmental dissonance.

Savannah and her friend Sofia were introduced in Chapter 2. They both had attended Latimer, the small liberal arts college. Twenty years later, when they are colleagues working in the same school, Savannah learns that Sofia is bilingual. In college, they both had climbed a ladder of inference: Savannah assumed that with a flawless English accent, Sofia must be a Hispanic woman who did not speak Spanish. She knows a number of them; they gave up their Spanish, like the Guatemalan child, in order to fit in. Sofia also climbed a ladder of inference by assuming that her English-speaking friend knew no Spanish and was not interested in learning it. Because Savannah is in the dominant culture, she has had the privilege of not knowing; as a result, both women lost the opportunities of deepening their relationship by learning about the other's ethnic culture, enriching their work environment by norming bilingualism, and moving from code switching to code sharing.

Now, Savannah is happy to practice her Spanish with Sofia, and Sofia comfortably shares stories about her life and family with Savannah. In college, a good part of Sofia's culture and worldview had been hidden from and marginalized by Savannah's privilege. Sofia's code switching skills enabled her to assimilate. Savannah's privilege kept her from learning any of Sofia's cultural codes. In college, Sofia code switched to fit in; now as colleagues, both women code share.

In Chapter 2, Peter, Dean of Advancement at Latimer College, and his new friend Aliyah, exemplify how moving from code switching to code sharing enable the Fish Out of Water to thrive in their environments. Both Peter and Aliyah are affirmed and transformed because of their openness to learn and to use new codes. Their goals are to thrive in both cultures and their openness allows them to do just that.

Also in Chapter 2, you met a professor who dramatically code switched as he moved from a presentation to his colleagues at the college to a pick-up game of basketball in the neighborhood. He contributes to a Culturally Proficient environment by code sharing. He befriends and mentors several of the young men he has met on the basketball court. He knows their codes and teaches them the codes of the university. He continues to learn from and about the young men while he helps them to navigate the path to success at the university. Additionally, he helps his colleagues understand the lives of the young men and how their cultures enrich the campus atmosphere. One result has been that several new courses have been added to the curriculum, all of which further share codes across cultures: Hip Hop and the Greek Chorus, Oral Narratives: The Griot in American Immigrant Culture, and Community Sustainable Agriculture and Urban Economies.

Thrivability Skills

Each person in the examples provided made choices about what they were willing to learn and to teach. Their choice to survive, maintain, or thrive placed them at different points on the Continuum. Each example points to specific thrivability skills:

- Identify the consequences of fitting in
- Resist conformity for comfort's sake
- Distinguish one's personal values from those of the environment
- Discern the codes of the environment

- Clarify and pursue a course that is in alignment with one's personal values and goals
- Learn from mistakes—one's own and others'

THE CONSEQUENCES OF FITTING IN

The row added to the chart in Chapter 4 described the effects of the different climates along the Continuum on beta cultures: alienation, marginalization, dualism, negotiation for acceptance, and transformation. Figure 5.1 summarizes the consequences of trying to fit into a culture. The Fish Out of Water have goals that change as the organizational climate becomes healthier. When the culture is described on the unhealthy, left side of the Continuum, the goal of the Fish is to survive; when the culture can be described by the healthy, right side of the Continuum, the goal of the Fish is to thrive. When the culture is characterized by Cultural Reduction or Cultural Pre-Competence, the Fish Out of Water are in a maintenance mode—no great danger, and no significant health.

In Figure 5.1 two more rows have been added. One row describes the goal of the betas and the other describes the betas as they learn and use the codes of the alpha.

When the *culture is destructive*, the goal of the beta is to survive. The Fish Out of Water buffer themselves against the destructive dominant culture by creating psychological and physical space between themselves and the dominant group. Minority groups isolate themselves, because they do not want to experience violence of any type.

When the *culture is intolerant*, the goal of the beta is to be tolerated. They know they are unwanted, and they know though oppressed they will not be eliminated—at least not physically. In this climate, the response of the Fish Out of Water may be to mask themselves. They wear masks that hide their differences from the oppressors in the dominant culture. They have to code switch to do this, but the beta code is hidden from the alphas. The culture of the beta may be completely different from the alphas or anything the alpha might imagine.

When the people in a group are blind to differences, the *culture is reduced* to a common denominator that includes all aspects of the dominant group and none that reflect the unique aspects of the non-dominant groups. The Fish Out of Water may code switch in the presence of the dominant group, but use of different codes is deemed wrong and punished or dismissed as having no meaning or value. The Fish Out of Water is able to engage in the alpha environment but is not able to contribute much.

Once she has crossed over to the right side of the Continuum, the Fish Out of Water can begin to build bridges between the two cultures. The Fish Out of Water seek to be included but may have to negotiate for acceptance. The code switching skills of the alpha culture are limited, so true inclusion is not achieved.

By the time the culture is characterized as *Culturally Competent*, the Essential Elements are being used as benchmarks. The betas are engaging with the alphas in a manner that leads to equity. Codes of both the alphas and betas are being affirmed and shared with the other. The Fish Out of Water can thrive in this type of environment.

At the point of *Cultural Proficiency* on the Continuum, alphas and betas are thriving together as they transform the culture. The alphas and betas in the culture merge many of their codes into a third set of codes representing them all in an environment characterized by equitable relationships and equitable distribution of resources

GOING DEEPER

Reflect

- Tell of a time when you tried to fit in. Were you successful? What where the consequences?

Assess

Focus on a particular environment.

1. What do you need to have in order to thrive in this environment?

2. What do you need to do in order to thrive in this environment?

Discuss

- Tell a story of when you shared codes with someone.
- What codes do you know that are secrets, which you would not share with people outside of your group?
- Tell of a time your first or second impression was wrong.

6

From Code Switching to Code Sharing

In order to engage successfully in an environment, it is important to know and meet the expectations of the culture. The process of learning the cultural expectations, especially the rules that are only known by insiders, is called *decoding the culture*. It is a strategy that often results in thriving rather than merely surviving. People who care about the people with whom they have relationships are constantly checking for understanding, asking for clarification, redirecting and refining their communication, and learning new codes. They move from code switching to code sharing.

How Codes Are Learned

Cultural codes are learned from birth. Parents learn to distinguish the different types of cries from their babies. An astute parent can tell the *I'm hungry* cry from the *change my diaper* cry from the *pick me up I'm bored* cry. As the child matures and learns the codes of the parents, he adds an *I'm faking* cry, which will get someone's attention, to his repertoire. These are codes the child teaches to the parents. However, it is the parents who teach most of the codes of the native culture.

What most might call *basic civilization* or *basic child rearing*, others will describe as *basic cultural codes*. Parents teach the children the appropriate tone of voice for speaking to other children and for speaking to adults. They teach them how to hold eating utensils; they teach them the rules for sitting at the table. They teach them to toilet themselves and the appropriate language for announcing their needs and the various processes involved. The child who learns well when presented to the preschool or kindergarten teacher will be deemed well behaved and ready to learn the codes of the school environment.

After the home codes, the child must master the codes for school. At home, a child will be praised for announcing the need to use the toilet and racing to the bathroom. At school, the child learns that she does not announce her intentions to the class, she must raise her hand and ask permission to go. Often the permission is denied until the appointed time for going to the toilet. At home the child is praised for speaking up, and demonstrating his growing oral language skills. In school, he learns that there is a time for speaking and a time for being quiet. To speak, he must raise his hand to ask permission. He learns that adults are addressed by last names and that the tone of voice used to address the teacher may be different than the ones used to address parents or other significant adults at home. The rate at which a child learns the codes of this second culture determines whether adults continue to perceive the child as well behaved, respectful, and teachable.

There are also codes for interacting with the other children in the classroom and on the playground. As the children mature, these codes become more complex. As they advance from one classroom to the next, they learn that each teacher has a unique set of codes, and success in the classroom is determined by how quickly and how well the children learn the new codes. Code cracking skills mature if they are used routinely. There is often, however, a point at which the older child or the young adult decides that they have learned enough. They have their own codes of deportment and their own standards for determining what is appropriate in a particular environment.

This is the point at which they are chastised or isolated for not using the appropriate codes, or they stop assessing the environment to learn the new codes. If an adolescent concludes that there is no need to discern the codes of the environment or presumes that the codes are the same everywhere she goes, her ability to discern and appropriately use the codes in new environments decreases. She is going to be pushed to the edges of her pond, or she will leave the pond—marginalized as a Fish Out of Water.

This is also the point at which someone who knows the codes must intervene. Code-cracking guides may be peers, older children, caring adults, or supervisors—they are the ones who whisper to the potential Fish Out of Water, "This is how we do things here. You'll be OK as long as you follow the rules." Cultural guides, mentors, and coaches are important for teaching the nuances of code switching. While much is learned through observation and experience, simply practicing the codes will not be enough. Colvin (2008), Greene (2012), Gladwell (2011), and others have made it abundantly clear that it is guided practice that makes the difference. Peter, the Dean of Advancement at Latimer College, practiced the handshake he had learned watching African American men, but it was his friend Aliyah who helped him to understand when and with whom it was appropriate to use the handshake.

DECODING THE CULTURE

Learning to decode a culture is a natural, intuitive process for a young child. As adults and older children acquire the skills and values for reasoning, empirical data collection, and rational decision-making, their reliance on intuition decreases or disappears. This chapter describes the process of decoding a culture for an older child or an adult. Most Fish Out of Water use some combination of the following steps to decode the expectations of a new or changing culture.

If You Are a Fish Out of Water

> When decoding the culture, ask, What is expected here? What is meant by . . . ? How do I get. . . . ? I noticed you . . . What did you say? How did you make that happen?

Name the Game

The first step in decoding a culture is to determine what the game is. Ask for help with this step, because left alone, most Fish Out of Water get it wrong. They may think the game in the classroom is to learn as much as possible, when the true game is to make the teacher happy. At home a child in trouble may think the goal is to be good, when in reality it is to stay out of Daddy's way and not do anything to trigger his rage. In an office, the game may be to make the boss look good—which may not have anything to do with the tasks listed in the job description. After figuring out the game, then one must figure out what the codes are for that game.

Observe What Others Are Doing

Listen to the language that is being used and how it is being used. Notice what people laugh at, take seriously, and ignore. Compare the rules you know to the rules that are being revealed. Notice nuanced differences. Practice aligning your behavior to the new codes. Ask questions of those who seem to be accepted and admired. Go to the balcony to get a different perspective on the unfolding drama. It is exciting to watch a game from the sidelines, but you might be able to discern more of the codes if you have a seat in the upper deck, because you get to see the whole field of play.

Try It Out

People learn new codes best by trail and error. They watch and try things out. If it works they keep on doing it; if it doesn't they try something else. We interviewed a twenty-five-year-old Fish Out of Water, who described herself as having evolved so that she now has legs. "I can swim or I can walk," she said. When we asked her how she learned the codes of a new culture, she told us that she has come to rely strongly on her intuition. "After a little while I just know what I am supposed to do. I learn by osmosis. I pay attention. I wait to see who gravitates to me, and then I check to see if I like them. If I don't like most of the people, I know I am in the wrong environment. I notice the reactions of others and I notice my own feelings in different environments, and I notice when I am just grooving. After I think I have figured things out, I test it, to see if I am right."

Get a Role Model

Sometimes they get a role model—a peer in the culture whom they can emulate. Jim, in his first year of law school, was asked to explain how he so easily adapted to the new culture. "When I am in someplace new, I stand back until I can identify the alpha in the group. Then I go make friends." This is a great strategy for a confident extrovert.

Find a Guide

A less assertive person may be adopted by a native guide. In schools, this person is sometimes called a buddy. It is always someone who has learned the codes of the culture and who can articulate those codes to someone new to the group. Cultural guides are good at relationship building and move with ease within the culture. They are very observant, yet remain uncritical of others' differences; they are fluent, fluid code switchers. They are neither high-ranking alphas, nor marginalized betas. They share and interpret what is going on without judgment. A cultural guide could be a truth teller in the group, an exotic, or someone perceived as crazy. Because they see so much and understand so deeply, most in the culture keep a respectful distance from them.

Increase Awareness

Often, by the time a child is ten or twelve, she must be reminded that each new environment comes with a new set of rules. Many times, adults also need to be reminded that what worked in one setting may work against them in another. Every environment has rules, a set of codes, and if those in charge raise the awareness of all about the cultural codes—that they exist and what they are—it will help anyone who might be marginalized for not knowing the rules.

Develop Options

There is almost always flexibility within an environment for individual expression and idiosyncratic differences. Fish Out of Water sometimes fail to notice the point at which their individual expression has passed the boundary of the cultural expectation of their environment. When this happens, the cultural guide can present alternatives or help the Fish Out of Water develop alternatives that are within the bounds of the acceptable codes.

Reassess and Realign

Cultures are dynamic; the codes evolve and change. Fish Out of Water who thrive in their environments reassess the codes and realign their behavior to assure continued success. The question they ask is, "Has something changed in the environment that would result in the codes changing?" New teacher, new standards imposed from an outside source, an incident that required disciplinary intervention, an accident—any of these things could be the catalyst for changing the codes.

IF YOU MANAGE OR MENTOR A FISH OUT OF WATER

Explicate the Obvious

It is important to remind the Fish Out of Water that some rules are formal and others are nonformal. The formal rules are listed. They may look like *Be honest, Be respectful, Be helpful*. Sometimes these words must be interpreted: How honest? Honest about what things? What does respect look like here? When and to whom is help acceptable? While the answer to these questions may be *common sense* to some, to the Fish Out of Water, they may not be common and they will not make sense until explained.

Reveal the Hidden Curriculum

The nonformal rules are the unwritten rules or the hidden curriculum. Those things that must be learned in order to be successful but which no one teaches directly: use of humor, where to sit in the cafeteria, what kind of foods to use for a lunch prepared at home, acceptable footwear. All of these are proscribed by unwritten rules. Children who break these rules unconsciously may be subjected to avoidable ridicule and marginalization. Sulaiman and his brother, Shakir, learned a rule about names before they reached middle school.

Sulaiman, twelve, and Shakir, eight, jumped out of the family car at the suburban mall. They were going to play video games while their mother went shopping. She had just finished her goodbye litany, "Stay close to your brother; don't get into trouble; call me if you need me," as the boys listened impatiently and responded politely. "Yes, Mom." "Ok, Mom." "We know, Mom." Finally released, Sulaiman called to Shakir, "Come on, Bobby." Shakir, responded, "OK, Peter." Confused, their mother said, "What are you two calling each other?"

They exchanged a look and said, with some confidence, "Oh, those are our White names. That's what we call each other when we are in the mall." Sulaiman and Shakir had discerned a cultural code—in the suburbs, alone at the video arcade, they would attract less attention if they used names common to mainstream culture. What could be more common than the names of the brothers on *The Brady Bunch* TV program?

Use the Rules Consistently

Once a culture has been decoded, it is important to use the codes of the new culture consistently. Inappropriate code switching results in undesirable attention, because it confuses those in the dominant culture. Yancy and Sierra were the front desk security guards at a downtown office building. All day they guided people from all over the world to the correct floors, the parking garage, and out of the building. They did their jobs easily and in the lull between visitors, talked with one another. Their easy banter and comfortable laughter made their friendship apparent. Entering the building, a well-dressed Black woman simply observed them as she acquired the visitor's badge that would be her passport to the forty-third floor. On her way out, with a little more time, she examined the artwork displayed in the lobby and quietly watched Yancy and Sierra interact. There were fewer people in the lobby, and Yancy and Sierra's conversation had become more boisterous.

After a few minutes of unobtrusive observation, the businesswoman checked out at the front desk and bantered a bit with Sierra. As Yancy and Sierra called goodbye to her, smiling and wishing her a good day, she turned around and with her best stern-mom look, said, "Goodbye . . . and keep your masks up." Yancy and Sierra exchanged surprised looks, looked anew at the woman, and did not ask what she meant. Nor did they continue their personal conversation. They resumed the somber and detached posture of vigilant security guards. They had been using their personal codes inappropriately, and after being reminded by a mother figure, they pulled up their cultural masks and used the codes best suited for their environment.

Explain House Rules

One of the privileges of hosting a game, whether it is on a kitchen table or in a driveway under a basketball hoop, the host can decide what the house rules are. The host determines the codes for success. In order to have a successful game, you need to share those codes with all the players. It is equally important for the teacher or the administrator to share the codes of school and the particular classroom, and it is also important for them to know the codes that the children and their families are using. Sometimes the subtle differences in codes make a huge difference in the school environment. Kids must be taught the school rules, as they were taught the rules in their homes. This means teaching the subtleties and nuances of the code, not just the words for the code.

The codes include expressive, interpretive, and responsive nonverbal language as well as oral language. The codes also include use of space. Differences in codes may include words used and the tone of voice and emphasis of those words. The codes also include differences in values. In school it is not ok to curse—curse words are called bad words, foul language, dirty language. In a child's home culture, use of words like sh*t, d*mn, and f*ck may be part of the normal lexicon. If the child has not been taught that these words are unacceptable, he will be confused if punished for using them. If the teacher does not know that these words are part of the everyday home language, she will be frustrated when talking with the parents. She may want the parent to be outraged, and the parent may respond with, "What is the f*ing big deal? The kid was mad, that's what you say when you are mad."

If the teacher asks the child, "Are you allowed to use that language at home?" and the child says "Yes," the teacher should believe him. The approach in that situation is to explain the schoolhouse rules without judging the home rules. *In this school, those words are not allowed.* It is not even necessary to go to the parent. If the child says, "No," then the parent can be solicited as an ally to teach the child the language appropriate for school. Ann Lamott talks about teaching her child the codes for using curse words in public settings.

> My son, Sam, had these keys to a set of plastic handcuffs, and one morning he intentionally locked himself out of the house. I was sitting on the couch reading the newspaper when I heard him stick his plastic keys into the doorknob and try to open the door. Then I heard him say, "Oh, sh*t." My whole face widened, like the guy in Edvard Munch's *Scream*. After a moment I got up and opened the front door.
>
> "Honey," I said, "what'd you just say?"
>
> "I said, 'Oh, sh*t,'" he said.
>
> "But, honey, that's a naughty word. Both of us have absolutely got to stop using it. Okay?"
>
> He hung his head for a moment, nodded, and said, "Okay, Mom." Then he leaned forward and said confidentially, "But I'll tell you why I said 'sh*t.'"
>
> I said "Okay," and he said, "Because of the f*cking keys!" (Lamott, 1994, 13–14)

Teach, Don't Punish

Teachers and parents must learn the codes of the kids. Knowing the codes of the Fish Out of Water will help the adults help the young Fish to decode their new environments. The best cultural guides, which are important roles for the teachers to play, know the codes of at least two cultures—that of the child they are guiding and their own. Kids are targeted and retargeted because of ethnicity, social class, economic status, native language, family composition, and the judgments made or stereotypes circulated about them. Teaching them the codes of the environment they are in will help them to fit in and reduce the occasions during which they are targeted.

When Fish Out of Water do not learn the codes or interpret them inaccurately, they are often punished. When adults do not learn the codes of the Fish Out of Water in their environments, they may embarrass or disrespect the children (or adults!) instead of taking advantage of a teachable moment. On the other hand, the gentle, nondirective language of some adults may not be perceived as authoritative. Children and other adults may perceive the subtleties as choices rather than directives. Decoding the culture is an ongoing, reciprocal process. Some people might call it relationship building.

Evelyn's Story

Evelyn had recently moved to the mainland from a small South Pacific island. While fortunate to be in the continental United States, her family was struggling economically. Evelyn was trying hard to adapt to her school environment, where everything was new to her. Recently, the teacher talked to the class about wearing shoes appropriate for school. Evelyn knew that going barefoot to school was not allowed in the city, as it was back home on the island, so after dressing carefully, she slipped her feet into her zoris—very proper shoes for school. She was surprised when the children at school called them "flip flops" and hurt when the teacher sent her to the principal because of "noncompliance with the dress code." "The very next day, after I explained the rules, Evelyn willfully defied me by wearing those flip flops to school," her teacher had said to the principal. Evelyn was confused; she didn't know what she had done wrong.

People who care about the people with whom they have relationships are constantly checking for understanding, asking for clarification, redirecting and refining their communication, and learning new codes. They move from code switching to code sharing.

GOING DEEPER

Reflect

- When have you had to decode a new environment? How successful were you?
- Have you ever gotten into trouble or been embarrassed because you did not know the unwritten rules?

Assess

1. Do you have a process for learning a new culture?
2. Can you list the steps to your process?
3. What are your primary code switching skills?
4. Do you know which codes need to be taught in your work environment? What are they?

Discuss

- Tell of a time when you helped someone to learn the codes of a new environment.

7

Self-
Monitoring
When the Fit
Is Not Right

When Fish Out of Water find themselves in environments that
do not fit, there are a number of tactics for surviving. Thriving,
however, depends on how resilient they are and how well they
use the strategies for thrivability and employ styles of
influence.

KEVIN'S STORY

In high school Kevin was popular and was among the few
students who could move easily between social groups in his
school. Being an athlete with good grades and a charming
personality, he was the classic big Fish in a small pond. At the
university, his status was very different; he stood out now,
not because he was popular and accomplished but because

he didn't know the rules of engagement. He attempted to engage with the students from the dominant group by getting involved in social activities and attending school-sponsored events. He was clearly different from most of the others everyplace he went on campus; he was made to feel like a visitor rather than a community member.

Because Kevin was the first in his family to attend college, he felt pressured to succeed. He was afraid of failing and afraid to let his family and friends know that he was no longer as popular as he had been. So he created a mask of success; he gave friends and family the impression that he had mastered being a college student and was on his way to the greatness his family expected of him. Kevin felt pressure from the people on campus for him to assimilate—to change himself into the college student epitomized by the dominant group. He felt pressure from his friends and relatives to be true to himself and remain the Kevin they knew and loved. He felt pulled in several directions and not understood by anyone.

For many students like Kevin, survival means dualism—existing in two different worlds, each unfamiliar with the expectations or codes of the other. For some people, a dual existence is overwhelming, and they have trouble in both worlds. Others learn to code switch effectively while nurturing their authentic core. Kevin, however, will not be welcome in one of his worlds regardless of his code switching skills, and to survive there, he must present a false face. He is never going to be comfortable, so he must learn to survive in this temporary situation in order to get the credentials that will make it possible for him to ultimately thrive in another. His college years will be a test of his resilience.

GOLF BALLS, SILLY PUTTY, AND 'TOONS

Resilience is elasticity of character. Once broken or damaged, to move forward, people need to reconstruct themselves; in order to do that, they have to be resilient. Golf balls are highly resilient: The harder they are thrown, the higher they bounce. They can be lost or misplaced, but it is almost impossible to destroy them. There are many more metaphors for resilience—Silly Putty, rubber bands, Slinky and 'Toons are a few. While a Slinky stretches and can take some abuse, it can easily become twisted or broken with no more capacity to stretch.

Rubber bands work only when there is some tension— when they are stretched, their elasticity and strength can be determined. A rubber band can be twisted, stretched, and pulled; it can be used to hold things together or to propel things. Yet, once the tension is released, it snaps back into its original shape. If it is too stiff, instead of stretching when tension is applied, it breaks. As it ages it loses its resilience and it does not return completely to its original form but it still clearly will be a rubber band with definite shape and structure. Rubber bands will keep on adjusting, holding things together and snapping back to their original shape, unless there is extreme tension, in which case the rubber band will break.

Silly Putty, on the other hand, will take on the shape of anything it is in, yet on its own, it is just an amorphous mass with no resilience. It starts with no basic shape, so it has nothing to return to, and because it has no shape of its own, it never looks the same. Silly Putty can survive in an environment that is rapidly changing, but one never knows in what shape it will end. Silly Putty is flexible, pliable, and adaptable; but it is not resilient. If it is pulled sharply, it breaks. Resilient people may be a little snappy sometimes, but they will survive during change. People, who are more like Silly Putty, may appear to be adjusting, but without any external support they don't move and can't sustain the change.

'Toons—the characters in cartoons—are, at first glance, the epitome of resilience because they always survive the violence to which they are subjected. No matter how often they are smashed to pieces they reconstruct themselves and move on. They are physically resilient, but they don't have resiliency of character or intellect. They reconstruct themselves in the same way after each crisis—with the same flaws and with no apparent learning. They keep making the same mistakes; they keep getting bashed in the same way.

Resiliency implies the ability to reconstitute oneself amidst change and transitions—but with some learning. So in the midst of the change, it is important to nurture the character traits that develop resiliency: flexibility, open-mindedness, clarity of values, the ability to prioritize and reprioritize when necessary, focus on goals, and willingness to reflect upon and correct mistakes. With some resilience, a Fish Out of Water will survive in toxic waters; with a great deal of resilience, a Fish Out of Water will adapt and thrive. Some people are naturally very resilient; others find it much more difficult to bounce back after a setback or disappointment. We are not sure whether resilience can be taught or developed, but we do know that adults and children can be encouraged to respond to situations in a way that reflects a resilient character (DeAngelis, 2014).

Tamarra's Story

Tamarra grew up as an introvert in a family of extroverts. She was an intuitive artist in an environment of thinkers and data gatherers. She knew what she knew, although her family often tried to prove she was wrong. She would come to an understanding of something intuitively, and because she couldn't say she had read it somewhere or someone had taught it to her, she—and her knowledge—was dismissed. So Tamarra learned to keep her mouth shut. She didn't talk much or often. It took her a long time to find her voice, to speak with confidence, to be the dissenter in the group, and to walk to the margins instead of being pushed there.

Tamarra resists oppression, questions authority, and is perceived as a nonconformist. She thought everyone should be outraged by the problems and contradictions that she saw in the world. Her friends and family thought she was being difficult on purpose. In her early years, no one, including Tamarra, knew that she was seeing the world differently. As a result, she stayed frustrated and angry. In that anger, in the midst of her outrage, in the depths of the despair at how helpless and hopeless she felt to be "the only one" who experienced the world as she did, she lost her ability to influence her environment. She gave her power away.

It is hard to feel one's power when one is gasping for survival as Fish Out of Water. Tamarra could not force people to like her, to include her in a sincere and authentic way, or to share power with her. Resilience helped Tamarra to survive in unfriendly waters until she could move away from her family to a more suitable pond. Using these thrivability tactics helped her to make a contribution where she was and in the new ponds she traveled to.

Tactics for Thrivability

These strategies enable a Fish Out of Water to thrive in and out of toxic environments.

Learn to Recognize Your Tribe

Learn to recognize your people, your tribe. If your people are not at work or school, perhaps you will find them in other environments. It could be your family, a social club, an athletic team, or just a few people you know. Belonging is important. You may not belong to the group you want to be with, but you can be with a group that wants you to belong to them.

Accept Your Difference

Get comfortable with your own style. Know your gifts and what you can contribute to the group; voluntarily offer these things. Celebrate your difference—not by flaunting but by being comfortable with your own style. Use your differentness strategically. If, for example, you are a truth teller, people won't want you around all the time, but they will come to you when they want to know the truth. If you are an exotic, you may not be invited to participate in public events; this may give you the freedom necessary to dress and speak as you desire.

Remember You Are Perceived as a Guest

Recognize you will never be like those in the dominant group; don't try to be one of them, just work to be comfortable among them. They may treat you like one of them only as long as you act and talk like them. This may mean you must buffer yourself against their micro-aggressions. Belonging as a welcomed guest rather than a shunned outsider may be your only alternative.

Resist Conformity for Conformity's Sake

Notice what you need to be comfortable—for example, personal space, time to reflect, freedom from micromanagement. Learn the rules and cultural expectations of your environments and show your respect for them. Now if you break the rules, it is not by accident. Learning to code switch will enable you to contribute to and receive from the environment, but if you are in the wrong pond, you will never be like the other Fish. And the mask of assimilation may begin to chafe.

Remember the Value of Community

Make small, noticeable concessions that demonstrate you are trying to use the codes of the culture. Ask questions that show you are interested in others. Stay away from "why" questions, they are usually received as criticism. Say, "Help me understand how *xyz* works. . . . " Surface changes are effective: Look the part. Kathy worked and was able to fit in at both IBM and Apple. The culture at IBM, she said, was pumps and pearls; Apple was a jeans and sneakers culture. Kathy was comfortable in both, and her expansive wardrobe served her well.

Be Clear About What You Want

Be clear about what is reasonably possible to get from the environment. Make it clear that you will deliver what is expected but that how you deliver may not be what is expected. Distinguish in your mind the difference between the rules of this environment and what you think the rules of this environment ought to be.

Understand the Advantages and Disadvantages of Being Different

If the authorities in the environment know that you are different, then their expectations of you will differ from their expectations of others. This may sometimes work to your advantage, giving you the freedom to respond to environmental demands in a way that is comfortable for you. On the other hand, being different also means that you are more likely to be targeted and your differentness may attract unwanted attention.

Walk to the Margins

Instead of being pushed, don't try to force your trapezoidal self into the round mold of the environment. Do your job—be super competent if you can and keep to yourself. When you walk to the margins, you keep most of your personal power. On the margins, you may be able to form a school of support with other Fish Out of Water. Within a group that is safe, you can also help other Fish Out of Water to learn adaptive skills.

Learn When and How to Quit

Sometimes the cost of being in a particular environment is too high for your physical and spiritual well-being. Staying on the margins may be too confining for you; swimming in shallow waters may cause you to stagnate. Whether you are swimming in the center of the pond or closer to the margins, you still have to be careful if you are a Fish Out of Water, because there are predators on the margins too. When you do leave the pond, leave well.

Work on Healthy Habits

To stay healthy while responding to the pressure and stress of the environment, rest, exercise, and good nutrition are essential. Under stress it is important to attend at least to two of these things regularly. Recognize the things that trigger your stress. If just thinking about going to work or school raises your blood pressure or anxiety, it may be time to change environments. Develop and pursue personal goals outside of work or school.

Take Time to Retreat

Take care of your personal psychic space—your soul. Soul keeping requires time, discipline, and reflection. "Your soul is the container for the essence of one's self. It is sustained by one's values and one's spiritual practices. The soul is not a physical part of one's self, but sometimes it is felt physically. It is important to take care of one's soul, because a neglected or wounded soul is painful to be around and even worse to

Tactics for Thrivability

- Learn to recognize your people
- Accept your difference
- Remember you may always be a guest
- Resist conformity for its own sake
- Remember the value of community
- Be clear about what you want
- Understand the value and costs of being different
- Walk to the margins
- Learn when and how to quit
- Work on healthy habits
- Take time to retreat

have. On the other hand, a healthy soul supports a vibrant response to life" (Nuri-Robins, 2010, p. 18).

Assessing and responding to the environment appropriately is required for successful code switching. An appropriate response to the environment is not necessarily meeting the cultural expectations of the environment, it may mean responding in a way that will allow you to survive in an unhealthy or dangerous environment. It is important to know what is expected of you, so you can decide the best way for you to respond. Sometimes it is wise to just walk away; at other times it is necessary to protect your boundaries and fight for your principles and rights. It is useful, therefore, to know what the dominant culture is doing and what their goals are in response to you and other Fish Out of Water.

Figure 7.1 describes the tactics of the alphas as the environment changes from Culturally Destructive to Culturally Proficient. The tactics of the alphas in the Culturally Destructive environment are to destroy all differences; in a Culturally Intolerant environment the tactic is to dominate. In a Culturally Reductive environment, all differences: not a part of the dominant culture are discounted as inconsequential. The Pre-Competent alpha is aware that codes other than his own are being used in the environment and accommodates the betas by recognizing their codes and perhaps using a beta code as an example or in an attempt at humor: *Well, if we have water sports, we know that none of the Black girls will participate because of their hair issues.* In a Culturally Proficient environment, alphas make sincere attempts to collaborate with the Fish Out of Water and, together, they cocreate a culture where the codes of both alphas and betas are used.

How to Survive in
Ponds That Aren't Right for You

Most of the time, there is safety and power on the margins with other Fish Out of Water. At the edges of the pond live

Figure 7.1   Tactics of the Alphas in a Changing Environment

	Point on the Continuum	CULTURAL DESTRUCTION	CULTURAL INTOLERANCE	CULTURAL REDUCTION	CULTURAL PRE-COMPETENCE	CULTURAL COMPETENCE	CULTURAL PROFICIENCY
		Policies and Practices That EXCLUDE			Policies and Practices That INCLUDE		
Ch 7	**Tactics of Alphas**	Destroy	Dominate	Discount	Accommodate	Collaborate	Cocreate
	Goals for Fish Out of Water	Survival	Tolerance	Recognition	Inclusion	Engagement	Equity
Ch 5	**Response of the Fish Out of Water**	Buffering	Masking	Code Switching	Bridging	Code Sharing	Bonding
Ch 4	**Effect on Fish Out of Water**	Alienation Elimination	Marginalization	Dualism Dissonance	Negotiation	Affirmation	Transformation
		Surviving		Maintaining		Thriving	
Ch 3	**Description of the Climate at That Point**	The dominant group allows only the cultures of the alphas. Those attempting to use other codes are banished physically or metaphorically. They hide or leave.	The dominant group recognizes that beta groups may use other codes, but those codes are deemed inferior. The beta groups must use the alpha codes to engage with the dominant group.	The dominant group fails to acknowledge that other codes or cultures exist. Those who know more than one set of codes are often closeted. The dominant group, in the spirit of "fairness" and "equality," uses one set of codes—theirs—to communicate with all groups.	The dominant group acknowledges the existence and usefulness of codes used by beta groups. Members of all groups begin to notice when it is appropriate to teach or learn new codes. Efforts to respond appropriately are inconsistent and sometimes ineffective.	Both alpha and beta groups in an environment engage in processes to identify, teach, and learn the cultural codes necessary for effectively interacting with clients, colleagues and community.	All groups teach and learn the cultural codes of the others. As diverse groups coalesce into new cultures, all use new, universal codes effectively.

the Crazies, Exotics, Truth Tellers, and Outliers. There are also supporters and protectors, as well as change agents—the Paradigm Shifters and the Visionaries. None of these important contributors to the community live in the middle of the pond, guarding the status quo—instead they are on the edges where they can see into the center and out toward the horizon at the same time. They are able to make contributions because they are able to influence the environment in more than one way.

Most Fish Out of Water underestimate the amount of influence they have on their environment and the people in it. Everyone has some type of power; people often feel powerless because the style of power they choose to use is inappropriate for the situation or the environment. There are at least six styles of power or influence; most people use just one or two. Some people use their power abusively; others don't use their power at all.

STYLES OF INFLUENCE

Fish Out of Water are ineffective most often in their attempts to wield some influence because they try to use formal or positional power rather than relationship power. Positional power comes with formal roles and responsibilities. Administrators have titles that indicate they are in charge of their schools or offices; teachers have authority in their classrooms. Parents have the power over children in the home. These positions of leadership come with the authority to reward or punish for not doing what was asked. This is called coercive power. The most obvious and direct paths to wielding influence are formal and coercive power.

Fish Out of Water are often not in position of responsibility or find that they are ignored when they attempt to assert their position power. They are better served by using relational or tactical styles of power. They use a range of styles of influence that results in not giving their power away. Fish Out of Water have to be strategic about getting where they want to go. Most people want to take the most obvious and direct pathway; they lead with formal, position power. The people who are most successful leading organizations and influencing the groups they are in lead with their personal power (Pfeffer, 2010; Nuri-Robins & Terrell, 1987).

Information

Access to and possession of information is the power that comes from knowledge. The impact of information power is greatest when people want the information or perceive the need for it. People who use information as their style of power analyze facts, historical experiences, precedence, and theory. They seek to control their environment by identifying issues, clarifying questions, and describing systems and approaches. They communicate to inform and to enlighten. They exert influence with others because of special knowledge they possess that is valuable to others. Educators and parents tend to overuse information power. They think because they know something that their students or children do not those without the knowledge will pay attention.

While many people use information as their dominant style of power, the key to effective use of this kind of power is having control of information that other people want. Having the information is not enough; it must be information that others want or are convinced they need. Moreover, the amount of information shared and the timing for sharing it determine the degree of influence the person using this style will exert. Fish Out of Water often use this style ineffectively. Because of their position on the margins, they can see what others cannot or have access to information that those at the center do not have. Unfortunately, most people in the dominant culture do not want the information that Fish Out of Water have, even if they could benefit from it.

Charismatic

Charismatic power comes from being charming, using your ability to make people smile. It's the attitude of the great host, being accessible and inviting. People respond because they feel good around you. Followers of charismatic leaders identify with the values personified by these powerful people and believe in the vision the leaders inspire them to work for. Magnetic leaders are charming, enthusiastic, and optimistic. They provide hope and a promise of improved conditions. They are most effective when morale is low and people are in despair. Magnetic leaders give their followers something to believe in that is greater than themselves.

Many people downplay this style because they fear being perceived as seductive or manipulative. The gracious host and the patient parent are images of magnetic power used effectively. Fish Out of Water use this style to charm their way into the good graces of superiors or to charm their way out of trouble or unwanted tasks. Fish Out of Water can be charming, funny, or cool. All of these are uses of the magnetic style of power.

Formal

People who lead with formal or position power have an official title or role. Many of them think that is all they need. They walk around with a sign saying, *I am the boss of you.* Within any organization there are formal and informal leaders. Informal leaders influence the environment when they are not in positions of authority. Formal leaders may use other styles of power, but they also have legitimate power, the power that is derived from the position or title that they hold. Position power is used by communicating through proper channels, recognizing chains of command, and demanding loyalty and support for procedures. People may cooperate with leaders who have position power because they respect the office, not necessarily the person who holds it.

That is why position power provides continuity in a climate of instability.

Consider the change in an organization's climate when there is no head. With no director or chief, there is a general discomfort among the people in the organization, for they fear that without a formal leader the organization will not survive a catastrophic event. An ineffective person in the position is preferred to no one at all. Position power is most effective with people who want to know what to expect of themselves and others and who prefer to function within formally established roles, behaviors, and responsibilities.

There is power in the position of outcast. People in power have lower expectations for people on the margins; consequently Fish Out of Water can use their position power to be left alone or to underachieve. On the other hand, a Fish Out of Water in a position of authority is better served when using affiliation or magnetic power rather than position and information power.

Relational

"Do it because I told you to" is the message from someone with legitimate or position power. "Do it because it will benefit the group" is the message from the leader using affiliation or referent power. Relational leaders are easy to spot in an organization. They are the coaches and the cheerleaders in the group. People follow these leaders because it feels good to be around them. They make the group feel like a team. Relational power comes from the followers' desire to be associated with the leader and with one another. This relational power comes from engaging with the people, spending time with them, listening to them, sharing a bit of who you are. Basically saying with your actions: *I see you and I care*. People respond because they want to be on your team.

The people who use relational power express acceptance of and appreciation for the situation of others. They show sincere concern for the aspirations, fears, and hopes of the group and the individuals in it. They are powerful because they can rally support for the value and importance of a common task. Relational power is most effective with people who want the security, support, protection, and shared acclaim that group identity provides. Charismatic and relational are people-oriented styles of power and are often used together. They are based on a value for supportive relationships. Fish Out of Water can use this style effectively by gathering with members of other targeted groups or being protected by a member of an alpha or agent group.

Coercive

The product-oriented styles of power are formal and coercive. These styles are used by people with a high value for task accomplishment. Law enforcement officers, parents, and teachers exemplify the position-coercion style of power. Coercive power works best in a period of crisis. "Do it, or else," is the message of the coercive leader. Coercion is the power of violence or threats of violence—physical and psychological. The threat may derive from sanctions by the leader or be the consequence of doing nothing in a crisis. Coercive leaders exert their influence by setting goals and standards for others, offering bargains and exchanges, and establishing systems of rewards and punishments. People who want direction are most comfortable with coercive leaders. People who need direction during periods of crisis can also be influenced by coercive leaders.

Of all the power styles, coercion is used least by Fish Out of Water and most used on them. It is the style that confirms the most negative perceptions of power. The coercion may not be physical, but it can create psychological pain. Coercive power is used to separate Fish Out of Water from the group. It is directed at the human need to belong and to avoid pain. Coercive power is overused in a culturally destructive environment. People with coercive power usually also have the power to reward; unfortunately, that side of this style of influence is not seen enough.

Strategic

An administrator who disapproves of the proposed project of a subordinate manager may verbally approve the action but prevent its implementation by demanding that first the project plan be presented for review, in minute detail, with a mountain of approval forms and signatures. This administrator is using strategic or tactical power. People using tactical power bring order and structure to an environment by developing systems and procedures, strategies, and plans. They marshal and monitor the necessary resources to accomplish their objectives. Fish Out of Water who use this style focus on problem solving; often the problem being solved is how to avoid being targeted by the alphas in the environment. Strategic power influences from the shadows; people get things done without getting noticed. It is creative power, recognizing that you don't have to go through the front door in order to influence what goes on inside. People respond as you desire but may not realize it is you who caused the rippling in the pond.

Sometimes the direct approach is the least effective for a Fish Out of Water. The styles of influence that are most accessible to Fish Out of Water are affiliation, charismatic, and strategic. These styles are the doorways to personal power—using the combination of personality, temperament, and situation to influence the environment or people in it. Figure 7.2 summarizes the six styles of influence and describes how it might be used in a power-filled way and in ways that disempower the user.

What style of power do you tend to overuse? With what other style might you be more effective?

Figure 7.2 Styles of Power and When to Use Them

Power Style	Power Full Actions	Power Less Actions
INFORMATION Use because you have special knowledge that others value.	• Find out what they want to know and do. • Connect what you are sharing to what is of interest to them. • Provide information in small usable segments, so they will always want more.	*Who Knows?* • Dummy up • Feign ignorance • Blackmail, extortion • "I know, but you don't." • "No one told me."
CHARISMATIC Use to nurture the feelings of esteem and respect people have for you.	• Use humor to connect with them. • Be pleasant and inviting, like a host. • Describe the inappropriate behavior and comment on how it may not get them what they want.	*Charming and Disarming* • "Do it for me, pleassse." • Cry babies • Femmes fatales, playas • Helpless, hopeless • Crazies, eccentrics
FORMAL Use to assert your formal position in the group.	• Agree with them and then direct them step-by-step until they declare that they can function without your micromanagement. • Acknowledge that they do not have to comply, but noncompliance may not get them what they want. • Teach what is expected.	*Authority Speaks* • "I'm in charge." • "That's not my area." • "I just got here." • Perpetual neophyte
RELATIONAL Use to draw people into the group.	• Use peer pressure to gain compliance—make the group responsible for the individuals. • Enlist the group leaders to bring in all the members of the group. • Establish relationship with individuals to show how much you care.	*The Gang is All Here* • "Let's make it unanimous." • "You're the only one holding us back." • "My powerful significant other would like . . . " • Would you organize a group to do this?
COERCIVE Use to offer pleasure or pain as consequences.	• Don't make idle threats. • Call their bluff. Offer to file a grievance on their behalf. • Clarify consequences: "No, I can't make you do that, but I can. . . . "	*Rewards and Punishment* • "Do it or else." • "You owe me." • "You'll be sorry." • "I can make it comfortable for you." • Bribes

Power Style	Power Full Actions	Power Less Actions
STRATEGIC Use to provide welcome strategies to accomplish tasks.	• Out strategize them. • Establish procedures and consequences. • Follow through consistently.	*Get Around THIS!* • "It's against policy, precedent, and tradition." • "We've never done it that way before." • "We've always done it this way." • "Put it in writing."

You may often find yourself in a pond that is not the ideal environment for you. This may be a temporary situation, or it may be a fact of your working (or social) life. While you most likely will survive in these inhospitable ponds, there is much that you can do to improve the situation for yourself. Your situation may not be ideal, but it will be much better if you develop qualities that increase your resilience, use a style of influence appropriate for the people and the climate, and employ the tactics for thrivability.

GOING DEEPER

Reflect

- Would you describe your resilience as Silly Putty, 'Toons, rubber bands, Slinky, or golf ball? Why?
- If not, what metaphor would you use? Why?

Assess

Are You in the Right Pond?

1. Is your current pond a good fit for you?

2. How do you know?

3. How do you come to understand the cultural expectations of your environment?

4. How close are you to the margins?

5. Are you thriving, struggling, or surviving?

6. Do you know who the predators are in your environment?

7. Can you protect yourself from predators?

8. Can you protect others from predators?

9. Do you know how to influence the alphas in your environment?

10. Can you engage with the people in power and the marginalized effectively?

11. Do you know their codes? Do they know any of yours?

Discuss

- What strategies have you used to thrive in ponds that were not a good fit for you?

8

Mentoring Kids Who Are Fish Out of Water

Kids who are Fish Out of Water get targeted, bullied, and ignored by both other kids and adults. Parents and adults who work with children must develop their radar for identifying the young Fish Out of Water. Small fry often do a decent job of coping, but adults can do a lot to help them move from surviving to thriving by teaching them to adapt, to be bicultural, and to code switch. Adults will also help by teaching everyone that dualism is painful and unhealthy and, in healthy environments, code sharing is necessary. This chapter may also be helpful for adult Fish Out of Water who are still mentoring their inner child.

Have you ever tried to open a door and cursed the key for not working, only to realize it was the wrong key? Have you ever managed to get in the car in the parking lot and then find it won't start—because it is not your car? Nothing is wrong with the key. Nothing is wrong with the door. Nothing is wrong with you—except—you didn't pay attention. You didn't notice the differences that made a difference. And yet, it is human nature to think something is wrong with the door when you do the same thing you have done in the past and, this time, it doesn't work. It is human nature to curse the key that no longer seems to work. It is human nature to say that children and youth, who are different—who are Fish Out of Water— are wrong, and if we fix them or, even better, if they fix themselves, they will be ok. Fish Out of Water don't need fixing; there is nothing wrong with them. When educators use the old keys with these kids, it does seem that something is wrong, because the old keys are not working. This chapter presents some new keys or new uses for old keys that may help the young Fish Out of Water swimming in your pond.

Backman tells the story of eight-year-old Elsa, who is chased almost every day just because she is different. Elsa is a smart, funny-looking kid, who speaks several languages and views the world through the filters of too-busy parents, who don't understand her, and a tough, doting grandmother, who does. Elsa is often in the principal's office for fighting. The principal tells her mother that Elsa should get psychotherapy or transfer to another school since she is so aggressive. When Elsa's mother asks why she fights so much, Elsa says it is because she gets tired of running. Young Fish Out of Water sometimes display behaviors that in isolation appear to be aggressive or antisocial yet, in the context of their worlds, are very appropriate. They are tired of running.

You can begin to help these young Fish with the words *STOP*. Stop talking about *those* kids. Stop thinking that you know enough. Stop feeling sorry for the kids you have not reached and then doing nothing more. When you hear an alpha make a comment that causes you to cringe, say "stop." When you witness children or parents being targeted with microaggressions, say "stop."

Khalil's Story

Walking to class on his first day of teaching junior high school, Khalil saw a kid who was his size—six feet of athletic muscles—with another kid half his size. It was clear the smaller child was used to being picked on. The bigger kid was holding the smaller kid by his ankles and bouncing his head on the pavement—the smaller kid's tears were falling up his face. Khalil grabbed the big kid and asked, "Why are you doing that?" With a slight shoulder shrug, his answer was simply, "I don't know." "Well, stop it," said Khalil. In that moment it was absolutely clear, Khalil knew he had to help the kids in his school who were being targeted.

Running away, running alone, or standing and fighting, a Fish Out of Water can benefit from having adults who advocate for them. A Culturally Proficient approach to helping young Fish Out of Water can be structured using the Essential Elements. The role of a parent or mentoring adult is to teach the child the culture of the community and help them to find a space for their individuality, creativity, and authentic beingness. Since many children are members of several communities, they may need several parental figures. The first parents may not know the culture of the school or the culture of the street. The second parents, those who are in roles of teaching, mentoring, and coaching children, are often the source of familial support. They may not have the child for twenty-four hours, but during the few hours they are with the child, they can teach cultural codes that will help the child to thrive in the new environment.

Using the Essential Elements

Each of the Essential Elements provides guidelines for a specific set of strategies for teaching the cultural codes and assuring the safety of all who are in that culture:

- Assess Culture—Assess the environment.
- Value Diversity—Crack the codes.
- Manage the Dynamics Of Difference—Track down the predators.
- Adapt to Diversity—Adjust the pond.
- Institutionalize Cultural Knowledge—Mentor and coach.

Assess the Environment

To help the juvenile Fish Out of Water, the adults must be aware of their existence and must recognize how children become Fish Out of Water. Many kids are targeted

Figure 8.1	Using the Essential Elements to Help Fish Out of Water

The Essential Elements	Helping Fish Out of Water
• **Assess Culture** Identify the cultural groups present in the system.	• **Assess the Environment** Identify the Fish Out of Water.
• **Value Diversity** Develop an appreciation for the differences among and between groups.	• **Crack the Codes** Learn and teach the codes that will enable the Fish Out of Water to be successful.
• **Manage the Dynamics of Difference** Respond appropriately effectively to the issues that arise in a diverse environment.	• **Track Down the Predators** Discern which people and groups are targeting the Fish Out of Water. Establish strategies for stopping their inappropriate behavior.
• **Adapt to Diversity** Change and adopt policies and practices to support diversity and inclusion.	• **Adjust the Pond** Begin the process of reshaping the organization's culture so that it is inclusive of all groups.
• **Institutionalize Cultural Knowledge** Drive the changes into the systems of the organization.	• **Mentor and Coach** Continue to work with the Fish Out of Water as they master the codes for success. Teach other members of the organization the codes for interacting effectively with its diverse members.

and retargeted because of poverty and ethnicity. Some have diagnosed conditions that make them targets, like Asperger's syndrome or cerebral palsy. Highly sensitive children and extremely introverted children get picked on by both other children and adults. A child who is the only one of his kind—his ethnic group, size, or ability, for example—may feel like a Fish Out of Water. Children with poor hygiene or with clothes that are very different than those of their peers often don't fit in and may be Fish Out of Water. Other young Fish Out of Water may be less apparent to the observer. Look for children who have no friends, who are always alone, or who exhibit behaviors that are overly affectionate or alarmingly detached from others.

Attitudes about and expectations of the children in a classroom can determine the extent to which they are marginalized and whether they thrive or fail. The most toxic place on a school campus is often the teacher's lounge, where information and judgments about students and their parents are generously shared, reflecting attitudes that may limit the development of children and create distance between the school and the child. Teachers' opinions and expectations are major factors in the success of students. When misinformation about kids is reinforced by other adults, when children are treated as stereotypes instead of individuals, children are targeted with micro-aggressions and micro-assaults that undermine student access and achievement. Instead of examining the efficacy of their own practices, teachers often conclude that something is wrong with the child and treat them like Fish Out of Water. They say, *Those kids can't learn. I've got one kid with a bad attitude. My class is great this year, except I have a few of those kids. Our scores would be great if we could get rid of those kids.*

Crack the Codes

Those kids can be of a different class, ethnicity, language group, or social group. They may be the foster kids or the kids whose parents are in prison or the homeless kids or the kids who recently immigrated to the United States. All of those kids are isolated by teachers' expectations. Schools are harmful places when a student is isolated. These students don't know, nor are they taught, the codes of the environment that will give them access to it. They are less likely to join support groups because as targets they are wounded, perplexed, resentful, and vengeful. They protect themselves with attitudes deemed adversarial that create even more isolation and negative responses from their schools' adults.

For many isolated or marginalized students, school becomes a place to be targeted or rendered invisible. Rather than being a source of academic and social development, school becomes a place to hide in fear of emotional or sometimes physical assaults. Most Fish Out of Water are unable to engage positively because they don't have the right mask to hide behind or they create a mask that hides them so well from their predators that they are hidden from teachers, mentors, and protectors as well. The results are poor achievement, disruptive behavior, and worse. Therefore, in addition to assessing the environment for Fish Out of Water, adults who care about kids must assess the environment for its support to predators who make the environment toxic with their micro-assaults and other marginalizing tactics.

The school culture is complex; the environment is created by a number of influences. Some aspects of the environment are systematic and structural—for example, how classes are arranged and scheduled, housing, and neighborhood conditions. Other aspects of the environment are traditional or associated with a particular school or organization—for example, how teachers are trained, how rules are created and discipline is applied, and how parents are engaged. Climate determinants also include the perception of and stereotypes used by the dominant culture. For example, many teachers judge parents harshly if they do not respond to notices sent home or cannot attend meetings the teacher has scheduled for them. We heard one teacher say, "That woman is a terrible parent. She needs to quit one of her jobs so she can make it to the parent teacher conferences." And some rules of the environment are idiosyncratic, tied to the temperament and personality of a particular educator or adult in authority.

All of these aspects of the school environment must be considered when identifying the codes that the child must learn. The basic questions to answer are, *What is the game?* and *What are the rules?* When the child does not appropriately respond to the codes of his environment, he gets targeted. Adults in positions of authority often misread student behavior as defiantly disrespectful when it doesn't match their personal expectations of how a young person should act. This is especially true when the student is perceived as someone who doesn't really belong—an outsider.

Track Down the Predators

It is human nature to isolate and shun those who are different. Some students are routinely marginalized by the dominant school culture, because members of dominant culture are fearful and xenophobic. Other groups, like gangs and cliques, marginalize themselves and may contribute to an unsafe or unhealthy school climate. Adults must learn to discern the difference between groups that provide beneficial support to one another and the school culture and groups that bully and oppress. Sometimes these groups, which have been routinely marginalized or isolated, do both.

Fish Out of Water who are obviously different from the norm sometimes make the Fish who belong to the environment uncomfortable. These Fish Out of Water, then, get targeted and bullied by both children and adults. So adults, the keepers of the culture, must develop their radar for identifying the young Fish Out of Water and consistently promote values that will keep the environment from becoming toxic. With teaching, mentoring and coaching, most Fish Out of Water can learn to function well in a variety of environments, and with appropriate monitoring, Fish from the dominant culture can be deterred from their bullying. The younger child in Khalil's story, at the beginning of this chapter, might never be an alpha in his environments, but he might develop the verbal skills or running ability to keep him from being an easy target for bullies.

During a faculty meeting, Patrick, the middle school principal, painstakingly shared suspension data with the teachers. "Twelve per cent of our students are Black and Brown, and last year, 40% of the suspensions were Black and Brown males. We have begun to address the problem," Patrick reported, "primarily by sending students back to the classroom for you to handle there. This year, the suspension rate for these kids is down to 25%. An improvement, but we still have a long way to go."

"We can get the numbers down even more," shouted a voice from the back of the room, "if we get rid of those kids."

Attitudes about children, like those of the teachers at Patrick's school, can determine the extent to which children are marginalized or made to feel at ease in the pond where they reside. Teachers sometimes misread student behavior as defiant when it doesn't match their expectations for "courtesy" or "respect." This is especially true for Black and Hispanic males. They are often labeled as "willfully defiant," noncompliant, disrespectful, and difficult for behaviors that are acceptable from other students. Black and Hispanic males in particular are labeled because they use codes that make the adults uncomfortable. Because educators do not have a diverse repertoire of intervention skills, these young men become Fish Out of Water and often, Students Out of School (Howard, 2010).

Just as children are taught to assess their environments and learn the appropriate codes, adults in the environment must relearn strategies for communication, discipline, and support of their young Fish Out of Water. Often adults participate in the bullying of children with the micro-assaults that result from responding to stereotypes and partial information. Protectors of the Fish Out of Water must learn to identify and redirect these adults or remove them from the environment.

SHERRI'S STORY

Principal Sherri had gathered a small group of boys into her office. These children had been a part of a rock-throwing incident. They had been seen standing on the elementary school campus throwing rocks over the fence at cars on the street. Sherri was in the middle of the listening session during which she invited the boys to confess to the part they had played in the incident. A teacher passed by the open door and stopped. Uninvited, she walked into the office, pointed to the one Black boy sitting at the table, and shouted. "He was the one. He should be suspended. He was throwing the rocks."

As the boy, cried "No, I didn't," the principal escorted the teacher out of her office.

In the hallway, Sherri asked, "Did you see Sadiq throwing the rocks?"

"No," said Jane, "but I know what kind of kid he is. I know he did it."

Sherri sent Jane back to her classroom and returned to the students. "Sadiq, were you throwing rocks?"

"No," he said adamantly. "I was there, but I didn't throw the rocks. I know it was wrong, and I didn't say anything, but I didn't throw the rocks. I just watched."

After discussing actions and consequences with the boys, Sherri dismissed them. She felt she had handled the situation well, especially with Sadiq. She believed him. It was unfortunate that Jane had walked by and tried to undermine her good work.

Her office manager walked in and quietly sat beside her. "Good work, boss." She said. "Now what are you going to do about that teacher?" Sherri's stomach flipped. It hadn't occurred to her that she needed to do anything with the teacher. Her job was to protect the kids. After a heart-to-heart with her office manager, she realized that she not only needed to address the inappropriate actions of the teacher, Jane, she needed to address the stereotypes and misperceptions of all her teachers in a professional development setting. If she focused on isolated incidents, she would unintentionally be supporting toxic attitudes that hurt everyone. Making it a school issue would reinforce for everyone how serious she was about her leadership mantra: Yes, all children can learn; now let's teach all the children.

Code Sharing With the Adults

Speaking up is a moral obligation. The office manager certainly had no professional responsibility to talk with her principal, but she used her relationship power to help her move the faculty toward healthier attitudes. She spoke up because she knew it was the right thing to do. She said, *I see you and I care*, to both the boys in the office and to her principal. The principal fulfilled her obligation to advocate for and protect the children in the school, even if it meant protecting them from their teachers. She was reminded that it was also her responsibility as an instructional leader to not just deliver inspirational platitudes but to provide a new lens through which the teachers could see their students. This requires teaching, not just telling. It requires that the destructive codes on the ladder of inference be revealed so that the teachers could create a new paradigm for what they saw when they observed the students. Just as important is remembering that it is the duty of the school leader or the leader of any organization to move predators—micro- and macro-aggressors—out of the environment so that they will not be a danger to the children.

Adjust the Pond

Care must be taken to ensure that the ecosystem of any environment supports the variety of Fish within it. Space for growth and proper nourishment are essential to the ponds' inhabitants. This means assessing the environment from the perspective of those who add to its diversity and making the appropriate changes. What may have worked well five or ten years ago may not be sustainable today, because the students in the classroom are different or the workers in the organization are different.

As a family grows and the members mature, the ways of doing things as a family change. The goals for each member's happiness and success may be the same, the values upheld by the family may be the same, but the strategies for reaching those goals change to accommodate the number of people and their changing needs.

In schools, the need to code switch falls more solidly on the teacher than on the student. Educators need to spend time with their students, in and out of the classroom, so that they can observe and learn some of their codes. Code sharing does not always mean that both parties use the codes of the other; it means that they notice and understand the codes used by the other. Teachers have the power to include or exclude based on their perception of the students' motivation and behavior. Understanding the culture and conditions of their students is essential if educators are to work successfully with them. In the classroom, teachers often make rules like: Show Respect. Be Honest. Stay in Your Seat. These words look good on the bulletin board, but unless the concepts are taught, they may not have any significant meaning to the children. Most teachers make the rules and do not teach the rules. Then, when a rule is violated, they punish children (and sometimes parents) for not knowing what they have not been taught.

Greene and Walker (2004) suggest that those teaching students to code switch engage in the following practices:

- Make certain teacher goals are communicated in a clear manner and that the students understand those goals.
- Explain how and when certain language—including tone of voice and nonverbal gestures—is or is not appropriate.
- Make sure students understand how certain contexts require code switching.
- Demonstrate code switching in the classroom.
- Affirm for students that their language and native cultural codes are viable and valuable.
- Develop culturally reflective assignments and activities with a focus on diversity.

Jameel's Story

Jameel is the oldest surviving son of a single mother. His older brother was killed, while sitting at the bus stop, by a random shooter a few years earlier. Jameel knows that his first responsibility is to be the man of the house. He has a commitment to helping his younger siblings and mother in any way he can. He is thoughtful, compassionate, and sensitive at home with his family, taking on tasks that are not expected of most children. This is what his mother expects and demands; she also demands academic success.

Because of his neighborhood, Jameel knows that he has to maintain a certain amount of "street cred" in order to be safe. His street persona is one of controlled emotions, challenges to authority, masked fears, and sensitivity behind a manly bravado. He walks tall, speaks with confidence, and shows no fear on the street. This attitude is not appreciated by the police. Because he is known in his neighborhood, he has been questioned as "a person of interest" on a number of occasions.

Jameel's mother is worried that she will lose another son. She has asked her older male relatives to talk with Jameel about the need to behave appropriately when he encounters law enforcement. This appropriate behavior—deference and submission—requires Jameel to employ different codes than the ones he currently uses. He already wears a mask on the street; the need to wear another inauthentic mask creates a major conflict for Jameel. He feels that he has to code switch too often. He wants to fight all the time, but the men tell him he has to be less sensitive and choose his battles strategically.

Jameel has to learn the codes of four different environments—school, home, peers, and police. He has different teachers for each of those environments. Men who taught about police were cultural guides. They would teach him other lessons about being a Black man in the United States over time. These lessons also taught him how to relate to his street peers and their demands. The codes of the school and home are significantly different and, in most ways less crucial, for personal safety. They are, however, very important to Jameel's academic success. All of these lessons help Jameel to thrive in his various ponds.

Mentor and Coach

In order for adults to help Jameel, they must understand his world and at least know the codes of the environment in which they interact with Jameel. Adults can teach about code switching and help the young Fish Out of Water to practice their code switching skills. They identify the basic codes to learn and how they apply to various situations. These are some of the many things that young Fish, especially Fish Out of Water, need to learn. They are survival strategies for life in a world that is uncomfortable with difference.

Howard Stevenson (2014) has developed a protocol for engaging with boys using basketball, martial arts, and other activities to assess how the boys might deal with interpersonal conflicts.

> Once he and his team get a read on boys' reactions and styles, they teach them more savvy ways of

addressing conflict. These include identifying their own stress levels, locating that stress in the body, communicating their feelings, and seeking to gain composure through breathing techniques that help them face the situation more calmly. A signature communication tactic is helping boys develop what Stevenson calls "the healthy racial comeback line," where they use wit to address tense situations but still make their views known. (p. 54)

Using the word play of Black youth to help them cope with life in public schools is not new. Playin the dozens, rappin, and other forms of hip-hop culture have been incorporated into many curricular areas, particularly oral language development, social studies, and music (Kochman, 1972). This form of code sharing allows the youth to use something familiar to them in new ways and to be acknowledged by the dominant culture. It also teaches the other students forms of communication to which they otherwise might have no access. Stevenson says his intervention strategies have increased rates of homework completion, reduced fighting and aggression, and increased anger awareness.

Understanding the Fish Out of Water and the additional challenges they face will change the way adults parent and teach. In addition to organizational and systemic changes, it is also important to connect to individuals. Just one sincere relationship can make the difference in surviving or thriving. A small circle of friends, even if they all are perceived as odd, can help the Fish Out of Water. While the small group may also not fit into the dominant culture of the school, there is some comfort in knowing that one is not alone. The outcasts of the dominant groups are role models for many.

Mentors teach survival strategies that help to keep Fish Out of Water viable when the environment is changing too slowly for life in a world that is uncomfortable with difference.

This is neither an ideal situation, nor the goal. It is the water in which young Fish Out of Water are swimming—today.

- *Be proactive.* Work to create safer organizational cultures where predators are not encouraged by your silence.
- *Be fair.* Recognize the difference between equality and equity.
- *Keep your expectations high and your ego low.* It is critical that all children are expected to achieve, even if all do not show gratitude for your codes haring.
- *Be honest.* Children must understand that they might always be different; everyone won't like them or want to be around them.
- *Develop resilience.* Enable young people to adjust to, adapt to, and recover from change, personal trauma, and the dramas of their life.

What Else You Can Do

These techniques are more nuanced code switching techniques that the young Fish Out of Water must learn.

Mask Up. Mask Down.

It is often necessary to wear a mask, to hide some of who you are, so that those you are with are comfortable with you or to protect yourself from those around you. Physicians, psychologists, and preachers that we know often talk about never sharing with fellow airline travelers what they do professionally. They put up a mask, saying they are in customer service or something vague, so that they are not bombarded with requests for free advice or inextricably caught in time-sucking conversations. This is mask-up behavior.

Wearing a mask is another metaphor for code switching. When the mask is down, the authentic self is revealed; when the mask is up, the true self is hidden and a face acceptable to the particular environment is presented. Basic mask-up behavior includes eye contact, shaking hands, and greeting adults (Johnson, 1971). These behaviors are part of dominant U.S. culture's native codes; they are what often are called simple courtesies or common sense. What is important to recognize is that the specific behaviors are determined culturally. What might be mask-down behaviors for members of middle-class, dominant U.S. culture, may be mask-up behavior for a student. It is not common sense or basic courtesy for everyone. Fish Out of Water and their cultural guides need to learn these things.

In order to not become a target on the street, Jameel wears a mask of bravado. When he is in school and at home, that tough guy mask must come down. His concern is that the masks he needs to wear are significantly different from one another and the consequences of using the wrong mask are many and life threatening.

Monitor Boundaries

When everyone belongs to the same tribe, they know the rules for the boundaries. In a diverse group, the rules for boundaries are as varied as the people in the group. Fish Out of Water must be taught about boundaries explicitly and experientially. They need to know what their own boundaries are and recognize when they are violated. Boundaries are both physical and psychological, and while boundaries are sometimes confining, they are also protective. Boundaries that establish personal space are as important as fences that protect one's house. Teaching about boundaries will include conversations about personal space and rules that govern what is OK or not OK to say to a child. Children must learn to recognize microaggressions, because sometimes they don't realize they are being ridiculed. Children need to be helped to recognize established boundaries and to know when they have overstepped the boundaries in a particular environment.

Read Nonverbal Cues

Imagine a young man and woman standing next to a wall talking with each other. Are they talking business or are they courting? Are they colleagues or something more? How can you tell? These nonverbal cues are called kinesics.

The most important kinesic cues that require code switching are those that convey deference and submission. Generally, White middle-class children are taught to look adults in the eye. "Look at me when I'm talking to you," says the White father. Children of color, generally, are taught to lower their eyes to show respect. They may hear from a parent, "Don't look at me with that expression on your face when I am talking to you."

If they are being chastised, many children of color will bow their heads, look at the ground, keep a neutral expression on their faces, and keep their mouths shut. They do not speak or explain or justify. Even if the adult asks a question, they do not respond. They take the reprimand and, when dismissed, walk quietly away. They may be asked if they understood what was said. In that moment only, a few words are expected. The child may reply with a soft "yes," and that is all. In a U.S. classroom, this deferential behavior is interpreted as sullenness, disrespect, and sometimes stupidity. Fish Out of Water and their teachers need to know how these behaviors are interpreted across cultures.

Listen

Many young Fish Out of Water know when they are in danger. They may not be able to describe what they need, but they are very clear about what doesn't work for them. The adults in their life can be helpful by listening. Adults usually make too many rules for kids, so they can set aside the need to be in charge and listen to the young Fish; they will learn what they need to do to help.

Ellie's Story

Ellie always knew she was a Fish Out of Water, and she could tell immediately when she was in a pond that was not right for her. She was fortunate that her parents listened to her, even when they didn't understand her.

When Ellie was six, her mother, Joan, thought she should take Ellie to church. Joan had been raised as a Christian, and her husband was Jewish, so they took Ellie to a number of churches to try them out. After several months of shopping, Joan decided to expose Ellie to the Catholic Church. They arrived on the day the children were learning about the Resurrection. This was unfortunate, because Ellie's grandmother had recently died, and so Ellie knew that being dead was not being asleep and that if you were dead, you didn't get up.

It was fortunate that Joan stayed with Ellie during the lesson. "Dead is dead, right Mommy?" exclaimed Ellie, in the midst of the lesson.

"Yes," said Joan. "But this is a miracle."

"No, it can't be a miracle; dead is dead. The teacher is wrong; I don't want to stay here."

So Joan and Ellie left, but decided to give it another try the next Sunday.

This time, Joan went to the service with the adults, and Ellie stayed in Sunday school by herself.

Joan's intuition prompted her to leave the worship service early to check on Ellie. She found Ellie sobbing in the hallway.

"What happened?" Joan asked, looking for visible wounds.

"I can't stay here, said Ellie. " I tried, but I can't stay here. This isn't where I belong."

"Well, we can go," said Joan. "Then we can talk about where we will go next week."

"Noo," wailed Ellie. "I just want to go back to our church."

"Which one is our church?" asked Joan. By this time, they had been to many churches on their church-shopping travels.

Ellie's response was simple, "The one where I belong!"

It didn't take long for Ellie to describe to Joan which church belonged to them. What she said was "the church with the big tree that has a swing." This was not, however, the reason that Ellie felt at home there. Her reasons were too sophisticated for her six-year-old vocabulary, but Ellie knew where she fit. And Joan had already learned that her extraordinary daughter would give her many cues for parenting if she just listened to her. Ellie is now thirteen and still very happy attending the church where she knows she belongs.

Giving Directions

The brand new second-grade teacher was frustrated, again. She had just told the children to go to their reading groups, and no one had moved. "What did you say?" asked her mentor, once they were in the teacher's lounge.

"I said, 'Would you like to move to your reading groups now?' And they just ignored me."

The kids misinterpreted the gentle, nondirective language of the teacher; she asked a question when she should have made a statement. She needs to learn the codes of the kids, and they need to learn hers. Given that the teacher is the alpha in the room, rather than punishing the kids for what she interpreted as disobedience she simply needs to teach them. "When I say xxx, that means you should yyy . . . " If the children perceive a conflict, she responds by helping them understand that as they move from the domain of one adult to another, the rules will change and they must learn what those rules are.

How a question or statement is perceived depends on the language used and the power differential between the speaker and the listener. Figure 8.2 shows how a simple question can be interpreted and misunderstood based upon

Figure 8.2	How Power Differentials Change Meaning

Statement or Question	Adult to Adult Meaning	Adult to Child Meaning	Child to Adult Interpretation
How do I get downtown?	A request for directions	A test for knowledge	A plea for help
Do you know how to get downtown?	A query that may be followed by a request	A question that implies a judgment from the adult—that is, you should know how to get downtown, but you probably don't, so you need to be quiet so I can tell you how	A challenge to the knowledge the adult has
Tell me how to get downtown.	A request from a familiar	A demand from someone with more power	An insolent request. Considered most appropriate and deferential is *Will you please tell me how to get downtown?*

who is asking the question and their power differential with the listener. Help Fish Out of Water understand the impact of volume, tone of voice, and facial expressions when there is a power differential. Fish Out of Water need assistance in discerning the codes of new environments and determining how to be authentic in a culture that seems to have no place for them.

Be a Friend

Sometimes a young Fish Out of Water needs an adult she can trust. The Fish may be a child who has been or is being abused. The child may be living with adults who are violent with one another and simply ignore her. The child may have a home life that is unstable and upsetting, or she may have had one single, terrifying, or traumatic experience, from which she has not recovered. The child may have withdrawn from her peers, finding safety in schoolwork and books, but be suffering from post-traumatic stress. Children like this have many needs, but the one thing almost any adult can do is to be a friend. Be the one adult who can be trusted, in whose company the child can feel safe. Be the friend who encourages, who inspires, and who listens; be the one who keeps the child from total withdrawal or decline. Many children who appear to be fine on the surface simply do not know how to get the attention from adults that they need.

Tochari's Story

In 1965, the following letter was sent from an honor student to the principal of a suburban school, her alma mater, in a large U.S. city.

I am Tochari. Archaeologists call us extinct. In places we are not allowed to live within the city—they run us out of town and we are told to live "out there" where there is no water, sanitation or housing; then harassed for living there plus called dirty. Some schools do not permit us to attend, and also refuse us a job and call us stupid. During World War II over 1 million of us died in the death camps but are not recognized as survivors of the holocaust. My ethnicity is also known as Black Russian, Roma, or Gypsy; yes, I am a person of color. I am Tochari.

I have harvested fruits, vegetables, and nuts, processed fish, picked up trash, washed laundry, pets, windows, and toilets in order to save money for college. In high school, two after-school clubs plus editor-in-chief of the literary magazine and choir events are all extra-curricular; my regular curriculum is honor classes carrying a

(Continued)

(Continued)

3.8 grade point average. I have aspirations, goals and determination.
I have received the female, Outstanding English Honours for my
graduating class of 600 students and am graduating number 25
in that class; but I have not even been considered for a scholarship,
grant or other assistance program in pursuit of a higher education.
Is it because I am a female? Is it because I am Tochari?

   I am Tochari. I am alive, not extinct. I am a young lady. I am an
honor student. I have the same educational needs and vocational
desires as other students. I have the determination to accomplish
them. What is it I must do to garner proper attention for occupational
goals? Please advise.

**In high school, she had been a Fish Out of Water and
ignored because she appeared to be fine. As an adult,
she remained a Fish Out of Water, who coped with
uncomfortable environments by being super competent.
She never got a response from her high school principal,
so in 1990, she tried again.**

I have diligently applied my efforts to the following: Graduating
from Oxford University with a Doctorate in Medicine, obtaining a
degree in Psychiatry from Stanford University, and maintaining an
association with Doctors Without Borders for many years. Presently,
I am retired.

   Students in the high school setting have personal obstacles to
overcome in addition to those that society and school presents.
Many times, just taking the time to recognize how hard a student
is attempting to complete his or her studies, deal with the
rigors of student social politics, or even blazing a path into the
upcoming world of adulthood could mean the difference between
a successful transition or a downward slide. Home life does not
always offer that necessary support. The journey through life
is both difficult and challenging, at best. Nothing can replace
positive support at a crucial moment in a teen's development;
without it, many lifetime emotional scars can result. I have
often wondered, how my life could have been different if the
administrator had replied, let alone acted, upon the letter sent
twenty-five years ago.

**Still no response and still smarting from
being ignored, in 2015 she tried yet, again.**

Awaiting the reply from your predecessor. At your earliest
convenience I would appreciate your personal response to that
young student of so long ago who sorely needed both emotional
support and financial assistance that was never received. I have
enclosed a self-addressed, stamped envelope for your convenience.

**Still a Fish Out of Water, this highly accomplished physician
continues to be rendered invisible and voiceless by the
administrators at her high school and by her colleagues—many
of whom think she is too strange to take seriously.**

(Shared in personal correspondence with authors.)

USING THE GUIDING
PRINCIPLES TO HELP KIDS

The Guiding Principles of Cultural Proficiency are the foundation for any intervention with adults or children. This is how the Principles would shape the language of an adult mentoring young Fish Out of Water.

Culture is a predominant force

We don't become aware of the water we are swimming in until it changes. Most people are not aware of their culture and their cultural norms and expectations until they find themselves in an environment that is different. Small children expect every place to be like home. Parents and teachers can assist in this culture shock by preparing children for some of these differences. Help them to anticipate what to expect and teach them the appropriate behaviors for the environments they encounter.

People are served in varying
degrees by the dominant culture

Expectations and perceptions of appropriate behavior are based on dominant cultural norms. While children may feel entitled do things in a manner that is familiar to them in known environments, they must be taught that the privilege of setting the rules shifts from one domain to another. When the child says, "Why can't we do it our way?" The easiest explanation is that everyone's rules are a little different.

We take our shoes off in the house at home. When we go to Grandma Helen's house, we keep our shoes on. At Nana's house we take our shoes off and she gives us socks to wear.

There is diversity within and between cultures

Help the young Fish to notice differences within groups as well as between them.

- *Even though we belong to the same family, we do not do things the same way. Auntie Sonia and Aunt Sierra are sisters, but at Auntie Sonia's, we say grace before we eat and at Aunt Sierra's, we don't.*
- *Even though you are at the same school, when you go to Mrs. Kenyon's class she will have different rules than Ms. Renee had.*

Every group has unique culturally defined needs

All needs will not be met by the dominant culture. Fish in non-dominant groups must learn to adapt and provide for their own unique needs.

- *I know you wear a scarf on your head when you go to sleep at home. At school when it is naptime, lie down carefully and don't worry about your hair.*
- *You do not buy your lunch in the cafeteria because we eat Halal (or we keep Kosher, or we are vegans). The cafeteria does not prepare the food in a way that our family has chosen to eat.*

People have personal identities and group identities

Teach the young Fish that there is a need for *groupies* and room for individuality.

- *Be the best you that you can be. You will be like some people and different from some people. Sometimes there will be a lot of people like you and sometimes you may be the only one like you.*

Marginalized populations have to be at least bicultural

Make the process of learning codes, code switching, and code sharing a normal part of being human.

- *No matter where you go, there will be rules to learn. Your job is to figure out what the rules are and what will happen if you don't follow the rules carefully. If you need help, ask a friend who seems to be doing it well or ask an adult to explain things for you.*

Families, as defined by their cultures, are the primary systems of support

Children may refer to family friends as cousins, aunts, and uncles. Not having a biological connection does not lessen or diminish the strength of the bond with the children to the people they call family.

- *I know your Aunt Althea is not your aunt, but she loves you like an aunt and that is what is most important.*

Each group's culture influences how problems are defined and solved

A child raising his voice and sharing his feelings with transparency may be a problem for a teacher but a source of pride for a parent who is teaching emotional honesty.

- *It's a good thing to be able to use your language to share your feelings. Remember at school your teachers don't always want to know how you feel, and they definitely don't want you to raise your voice when you tell them.*

GOING DEEPER

Reflect

- Think of a time when, as a child, you learned to code switch? How did you learn?
- How conscious were you about learning the new code?

Assess

Is This Child a Fish Out of Water?

1. Can this child code switch?

2. What codes does this child need to know?

3. Is this child aware that codes change from one environment to the next?

4. Does the child code switch between formal and casual situations?

5. Does this child code switch between adults and children?

6. Does this child have any friends?

7. Does this child appear to be isolated from age peers?

8. Is this child depressed or noticeably quiet?

9. Is this child able to hold a conversation with an adult?

10. Can this child distinguish between important details and unnecessary ones when telling a story? Is this child constantly seeking attention?

11. Is this child uninterested in school activities?

12. Has this child become less talkative than usual?

13. Does this child over explain things?

14. Does this child demonstrate a sense of humor?

15. Is this child highly accomplished and super competent?

Answering YES *to any number of these questions may signal a need for intervention for a young Fish Out of Water.*

Discuss

- Tell a story about helping a young Fish Out of Water.
- Tell a story about a child learning to code switch.
- What resources are available for helping the young Fish Out of Water that you know?

9

Managing Fish Out of Water

> The ultimate leadership goal is to systematically deconstruct dysfunctional structures and to remove all predators from the environment. Until this goal is achieved and every school in every district and every organization in every city is Culturally Proficient, managers must work, using their personal power, within their spheres of influence, to make the organizational climate healthier and to help the Fish Out of Water thrive by teaching, coaching, and shepherding them toward success.

The child who is targeted by classmates and other teachers grows up to be an adult who is a Fish Out of Water. The young Fish Out of Water who is too different to be accepted by his peers eventually grows up and remains too different to be accepted by his peers. Fish Out of Water of every age and in every type of organization are marginalized and oppressed by systemic structures and the actions of individuals. You may not be an adult who is a Fish Out of Water; you may be very comfortable in your cultural pond. You may, however, be the manager of a Fish Out of Water and not be sure how to help them.

As adults, they are not much different than children. They may be funny looking or funny talking, and they are slightly out of step socially. They are loners, too quiet, overly dramatic, too focused on details, too enamored with the big picture. Sometimes the Fish Out of Water lack emotional intelligence; their approaches to colleagues may be off or their reactions may seem inappropriate. They seem to disrespect the rules or ignore the way things are done with your team. You tell them what you want, and they insist on doing things their own way. They are a source of great frustration. This is the point at which we, as consultants, are called. "If she doesn't change," says the manager, "I am going to have to fire her."

Fish Out of Water can make a wonderful contribution to the work environment or they can be a nightmare to manage, and that all depends on the manager. Think about the people for whom you are responsible, and think about those who do not meet their potential or your expectations. Your Fish Out of Water are probably among this group. If when you are thinking about these people you reflect on the number of warnings you have given, the many disciplinary conversations you have had, or their remarkable absence of common sense or basic social skills, you have probably narrowed the field to the few Fish Out of Water you have.

Success in managing Fish Out of Water is linked to the success in developing a relationship of trust with them. A Fish Out of Water may be living a dual life. They may be closeted because of gender nonconformity. They may appear to be White but be a part of a multiracial family; this may be very uncomfortable for them if the environment is conservative or culturally intolerant of non-dominant ethnic groups. The Fish Out of Water you are managing may have a personality style or Myers Briggs Type (MBTI) that is rare in the general population or dissonant with the majority of the people on your team. Invisible handicaps, such as dyslexia or hearing impairments, may cause the Fish Out of Water to be out of step with the rest of the team.

The same strategies for mentoring and nurturing young Fish Out of Water that were described in Chapter 8 can be used for the adult Fish. The major difference is that adult Fish may not be as compliant, and the colleagues of the adult Fish Out of Water may not be as tolerant or as patient as they are with young people. Your first task, as manager, is to identify the Fish Out of Water, and your second task is to build a relationship, so that you can learn something about them. Once you have climbed down the ladder of inference and set aside your judgments based on stereotypes and incomplete information, you can start to find ways to connect to the person. Seek to learn their concerns, their goals, their frustrations. Share something of yourself with them. Build a relationship. After a couple of conversations, perhaps over coffee, you will have gathered some data and can begin to cocreate a plan.

In most organizations, after the first-week orientation, the new hire is on her own to figure out the norms and cultural expectations. An induction process during which the new hire is provided a cultural guide will insure greater success in learning the codes of the environment. When a new person joins the team, he or she usually is asked to *Tell us a little about yourself.* But the sharing is not reciprocated. At most, the veteran team members provide name and job title.

It is important to remember that when a new person joins the team the team process resets to zero, no matter how highly functioning the team has been. If the new member is welcomed into the group effectively, the induction period will be faster, and the highly performing team will restart and move forward relatively quickly. Relatively quickly means that the team will be high performing again in a much faster time period than if no deep induction to the groups' culture is made. It is important to include all team members in the induction process, because this is where the code sharing begins. Even when your team is excellent, there are still things that the team can learn that will help it to continue to be excellent and to excel in new arenas.

Learn some of the codes and cultural filters that the new person has and teach the codes of the team. This teaching may include some contrastive analysis. If the person has come from a large suburban school and is now in a small charter school in mid-city, there are many environmental factors that will be different. The successful manager will compare and contrast some of those differences, thereby helping the inductee to manage their expectations. This process is similar to welcoming a guest into your home when you know they will be leaving in a few days and helping a new family member learn how you do things in your home that is now also hers.

George's Story

George was the minister of music for thirty years at Great Bethel Church, until his friend and colleague, Tim, the senior pastor, died. George and Tim had shaped the culture of Great Bethel and had grown the roster from 300 to 1500 families. Everything changed after Tim died. The new young pastor who took over at Bethel pushed George out. Now George, bitter and frustrated, is looking for a new place to call home. He thinks he may have found it at Progressive Way, a church of another denomination.

The problem is that George is used to being in charge, and Progressive Way is much more liberal and democratic than Great Bethel. As they plan a special worship service, Barbara, who has known George for many years and worked with him at Bethel, helps to interpret to George the culture of Progressive Way, where she is now the pastor. George was a bit prickly because he couldn't

(Continued)

(Continued)

understand why a layperson was running the meeting and why he couldn't make the decisions about which music to use. Barbara explained to George how decisions were made at Progressive Way and modeled for the other members of the worship team ways of getting George's attention and cooperation, without frustrating him even more. The meeting was a bit tense and took longer than they had expected, but everyone was happy with the result—a great worship service, new music, and most exciting of all, a new musician.

USING THE ESSENTIAL ELEMENTS AS A MANAGER

The Essential Elements of Cultural Proficiency, which were introduced in Chapter 3, provide the standards for your work as a manager of Fish Out of Water:

Assess the Culture
Scan the environment to identify the Fish Out of Water.

Value Diversity
Learn and teach the codes that will enable the Fish Out of Water to be successful.

Manage the Dynamics of Difference
Discern which people and groups are targeting Fish Out of Water. Establish strategies for stopping their inappropriate behavior.

Adapt to Diversity
Reshape the organization's culture so that it is welcoming and inclusive.

Institutionalize Cultural Knowledge

Mentor and coach the Fish Out of Water as they master the codes for success. Teach other members of the organization the codes for interacting effectively with its diverse members.

What works and what doesn't work? For whom does the culture work? Notice who fits into the culture and who doesn't. Remember that the dominant culture serves its own best. Reinforce the cultural norms that reflect a value for diversity and inclusion. Nurture the diverse talent in your pond. Don't just state the cultural norms and expectations—teach them. Teach everyone skills to manage the dynamics of difference: communication, listening, problem solving, and conflict resolution. Create swimming and growing space for all the Fish in your pond. Doing nothing disadvantages everyone.

In a Culturally Proficient environment, all stakeholders engage in ways that say, *I see you and I care. I care enough to be curious about who you are. I care enough to learn to communicate with you. I care enough to tell you how we do things here. I care enough to adapt the way we do things so that they reflect you and your needs as well as mine. I care enough to share my codes and learn yours.*

There are people in the environment who remain unseen and voiceless—or worse—targeted and underserved because their needs are not being met. These are the people who have not figured out the codes of the organization or who, for a variety of reasons, don't fit in. People are served in varying degrees by the dominant culture, and when members of non-dominant groups do not know the codes or have not learned to code switch, they cannot participate fully or derive all of the benefits from being in a group. This is a problem for children, and it is a big problem for adults.

You may supervise people who don't quite fit into the organizational culture, because they have not learned to code switch in an environment that is ill prepared to welcome them. The Culturally Proficient manager will work with Fish Out of Water to help them to learn the codes of the organization and, during that process, will learn the codes of the Fish, so that they can communicate effectively. As protector, teacher, coach, and mentor, the manager of the Fish Out of Water assesses the person and the environment. Then you can clearly present your expectations for performance and the standards by which performance will be evaluated.

Within this context, the Culturally Proficient manager discerns the difference in the desire to tell and the need to teach. If something falls within the frame of common sense that the marginalized person doesn't know, then it is likely that these are codes that must be taught. If there are gaps in the professional knowledge or skill set, then these are areas for professional development and coaching. If there is great dissonance between the temperament and values of the person and the personality and values of the organization, then a conversation about the costs of staying is needed.

Sometimes the manager must determine that the fit is not right and help the person who is not meeting expectations to exit. Most of the time, this involves presenting what you perceive are options and then supporting the staff person as he makes a decision about staying in an uncomfortable setting or leaving. There is a great difference between an environment that is culturally destructive and an environment that is not a good fit because of significant differences in values or style. If the environment is destructive or intolerant, the environment has to change, and as manager, it is your job to lead that change.

On the other hand, a person would have to discern which organization, Apple or Microsoft, was a better fit for him. A teacher with extraordinary gifts and K–12 credentials would need to decide whether she preferred to teach social studies in fifth grade or eleventh. An administrator might work exceptionally well in a highly structured private college prep school and not so well in a progressive, open classroom charter school. Ideally, the choice to stay or leave should be about style, values, and temperament, not about the targeted status of the person making the decision. Even the best of organizations will not be a comfortable fit for everyone.

The Manager as Advocate and Coach

Figure 9.1 adds one more row to the chart you have seen in Chapters 3, 4, 5, and 7. In Chapter 7, a row was added that summarizes how the alphas respond to Fish Out of Water. The Culturally Proficient manager must be aware of these tactics, because in addition to coaching the Fish Out of Water, the manager may have to engage in redirecting conversations with mainstream Fish who are behaving inappropriately. In Figures 9.1 and 10.1 the role of this manager is described.

Remember that this is not the manager who supports the status quo; these two rows describe the behaviors of a manager seeking to nurture a healthy, diverse, and inclusive environment. Chapter 10 describes the approach taken to change the organization. Chapter 9 focuses on the role of the manager when he interacts with individual Fish Out of Water. As the environment improves, the manager is less of a protector and more of a mentor and coach. The manager works with the whole team, modeling a value for diversity and inclusion and fostering healthy code sharing.

When the environment is Culturally Destructive, the manager must protect the Fish Out of Water by teaching the marginalized person to recognize codes that signify danger and using the codes of authority and power to keep the danger at bay.

When the environment is Culturally Intolerant, the manager must identify the Fish Out of Water and induct them into the culture. The induction process includes teaching the codes of success in that particular environment and learning some of the codes of the Fish Out of Water.

Figure 9.1 Role of the Manager With Fish Out of Water

	Point on the Continuum	CULTURAL DESTRUCTION	CULTURAL INTOLERANCE	CULTURAL REDUCTION	CULTURAL PRE-COMPETENCE	CULTURAL COMPETENCE	CULTURAL PROFICIENCY
		Policies and Practices That EXCLUDE			Policies and Practices That INCLUDE		
Ch 9	Role of the Manager With the Individual	Protect	Identify & induct	Recognize & reinforce	Induct & coach	Integrate	Mentor
Ch 7	Tactics of Alphas	Destroy	Dominate	Discount	Accommodate	Collaborate	Cocreate
Ch 5	Goals for Fish Out of Water	Survival	Tolerance	Recognition	Inclusion	Engagement	Equity
Ch 4	Response of the Fish Out of Water	Buffering	Masking	Code Switching	Bridging	Code Sharing	Bonding
	Effect on Fish Out of Water	Alienation Elimination	Marginalization	Dualism Dissonance	Negotiation	Affirmation	Transformation
		Surviving		Maintaining		Thriving	
Ch 3	Description of the Climate at That Point	The dominant group allows only the cultures of the alphas. Those attempting to use other codes are banished physically or metaphorically. They hide or leave.	The dominant group recognizes that beta groups may use other codes, but those codes are deemed inferior. The beta groups must use the alpha codes to engage with the dominant group.	The dominant group fails to acknowledge that other codes or cultures exist. Those who know more than one set of codes are often closeted. The dominant group, in the spirit of "fairness" and "equality" uses one set of codes—theirs—to communicate with all groups.	The dominant group acknowledges the existence and usefulness of codes used by beta groups. Members of all groups begin to notice when it is appropriate to teach or learn new codes. Efforts to respond appropriately are inconsistent and sometimes ineffective.	Both alpha and beta groups in an environment engage in processes to identify, teach and learn the cultural codes necessary for effectively interacting with clients, colleagues, and community.	All groups teach and learn the cultural codes of the others. As diverse groups coalesce into new cultures, all use new, universal codes effectively.

152

When the environment is Culturally Reductive, the manager must recognize the diversity that is present in the environment and reinforce the value of diversity. Cultural reduction is dysfunctional to high performance teams

When the environment is Culturally Pre-Competent, the manager must induct and coach the Fish Out of Water. The induction process may last a year or more, as the new team members move through the seasonal cycles of the organization.

When the environment is Culturally Competent, the manager must help to integrate the Fish Out of Water into the environment.

When the environment is Culturally Proficient, the manager must mentor the Fish Out of Water, making sure that the code sharing is appropriate and sufficient.

Using the Guiding Principles to Help Adult Fish Out of Water

Adult Fish Out of Water often make faux pas that must be corrected, take actions that must be redirected, or need information that will help them stay connected. People who manage people who don't fit in must know how to help them. As you coach and mentor adult Fish Out of Water, your feedback and guidance can be shaped by the Guiding Principles of Cultural Proficiency. Quick intervention will keep these folk from being permanently marginalized.

Culture is a predominant force

Culture is everywhere, and you must recognize that in addition to the policies and procedures in the Personnel Manual, there are house rules for how we do things here. These unwritten rules may be even more important to your success than the written rules. We hired you because we believe you have the skills and knowledge to do this job. What you must learn is the culture here so that you use your skills while meeting the cultural expectations of this organization.

People are served in varying degrees by the dominant culture

It probably isn't a good idea to start every comment you make with, "At my last job we. . . . " Your new colleagues want to know that you appreciate who they are and what they do. Comparing everything to what you did before is telling your colleagues that you think what they are doing is incorrect or inadequate. You will be helping to shape the culture here, but first you have to learn the culture.

There is diversity within and between cultures

I know you were trying to be politically correct. I would rather you be culturally correct. You cannot tell people what cultural groups they can or cannot belong to. Yes. Lucia lives with a man. Yes. Lucia identifies as a lesbian. That's all you need to know. The rest is not your business. If you are curious, then you build a relationship with Lucia and ask her about it privately. Otherwise, keep your judgments to yourself. Meanwhile, if her community has selected her as a spokesperson, then you must yield the floor so she can speak.

Every group has unique culturally defined needs

As you know, we do not have a Kosher kitchen. I think though that we can talk with the food services manager about setting aside space in the small refrigerator for your lunch. There are probably others on staff who might appreciate a Kosher-only space in the kitchen.

People have personal identities and group identities

I am not sure if you identify as a woman of color, but if you do, there is an organization of employees who meet around issues for people of color. Here is a list of all of the special interest groups that I know of; you might want to ask some of your colleagues if you belong to a group that doesn't appear to be represented on this list.

Marginalized populations have to be at least bicultural

As you know from your previous jobs, everybody wants access to the IT guys, but most of us cannot speak IT. So that leaves the burden on you. We need you, we want you to help us, and you are going to have to translate your tech talk into language that we non-tech people can understand.

Families, as defined by their cultures, are the primary systems of support

Yes, we end the fiscal year with a family picnic. You are not required to bring family members; you may prefer to bring people who are not related to you who treat you like family.

Each group's culture influences how problems are defined and solved

Yes, I know you get your work done quickly. And yes, I know that your productivity is greater than most of the people in your department. I still need you to be here on time and not leave until the end of the day. Your routine tardiness is a problem for me, because it affects the morale of those in your department. So let's talk about how you can look more like a team player.

GOING DEEPER

Reflect

- As a manager, what are your best skills for helping Fish Out of Water?

Assess

Are You Helping any Fish Out of Water?

1. How well do your people fit in your pond?
2. How healthy is your organization's environment?
3. What do the Fish Out of Water in your organization need?
4. Do they all need the same thing?
5. What are your code switching skills? How do you know?
6. Do you know which codes need to be taught?
7. What evidence do you have of code sharing?
8. What is the formal induction process for your organization?
9. Is it enough?

Discuss

- Use Figure 9.1 to describe an environment you are a part of and strategies for assisting the adult Fish Out of Water in that environment.

10

Managing the Environment

The Cultural Proficiency journey involves the transformation of people and organizations, moving them from Cultural Destructiveness to Cultural Proficiency. You may choose from among many ways to take this journey. On your journey, you must find the work on which you will focus. You may choose to work to eliminate Barriers, to reinforce the Principles, or to target the standards reflected in the Elements. Some of you may help Fish Out of Water find the ponds in which they can thrive, while guiding those Fish who control the ponds to make them more diverse and inclusive.

NURTURING THE ORGANIZATION'S CULTURE

Nurturing a welcoming and inclusive environment is one of the fundamental tasks of a healthy learning community. If you are comfortable in your cultural pond, you are in a position to help others who are Fish Out of Water. If you are the manager of a Fish Out of Water, you can help this person to adapt, adjust, and thrive. As a leader, you can notice those environments that are ready for change, and you can help to make them safer for more people.

Creating a healthy organizational culture is easy when everyone is just like you, when everyone is on their best behavior, or when the diversity among the population is temporary. It is easy to be welcoming when the newcomers don't challenge your boundaries, your values, your practices, or your authority. It is not so easy when you are invited to step out of your box of comfortable paradigms.

Leaders of organizations can decide what kind of organizational culture they want. Is it an IBM type culture that is mature and relatively conservative? Is it an Apple type culture that is creative and casual? Schools make similar decisions, hence the plethora of magnet schools, charter schools, private schools, and public schools. However, once the core values of the organization are determined, every step must be taken for the culture to be welcoming to the diverse populations that are present or invited into that culture. Concomitantly, strong affirmative actions must be taken to redirect, discipline, or dismiss the predators within the culture.

As a manager, you may have to choose between the familiarity of a toxic environment or the discomfort of working to change it. You may be an alpha in the environment, or you may have learned to navigate the unhealthy waters; others may not be so privileged. Fish Out of Water who have not learned to code switch or cannot use the codes because they conflict too greatly with who they are may blame themselves because they have become targets in their environments. Others may accept their own differentness and accept the harassment that comes with it. Most become some combination of disillusioned, angry, depressed, belligerent toward others, or self-destructive.

A culture that doesn't allow its members to learn and grow from their similarities and differences is at best unhealthy and at its worst toxic; and a toxic environment is harmful to all the people in it. Indicators of an unhealthy environment include the following:

- Inequitable distribution of resources
- High rates of turnover and absenteeism
- Suspension and expulsion disparities
- High rates of disciplinary actions
- Low morale
- Incivility, bullying, harassment
- Inequitable distribution of power
- A homogeneous environment where there is no creative conflict and no challenge of the status quo

In addition to these symptoms, disaggregated data reflect a lack of parity with the population for people or groups that experience these symptoms.

Sometimes the environment is not toxic but is too small for the Fish who are in it. There is not room for growth or development. Healthy organizations demand an ongoing assessment of the conditions that support thrivability. How well does the environment induct new arrivals? How well does the environment adapt to change? What are the required codes of conduct, cultural expectations, and standards for communication? How do the attitudes and beliefs of teacher and staff affect student performance and involvement in community life?

USING THE VALUES OF THE ORGANIZATION

There are several approaches to nurturing a healthy organizational climate. One point of entry is through the organization's values and mission statement. Near the reception desk of every school, district office, and not-for-profit organization, a document is hung prominently that displays the mission or values. The mission speaks to the service that will be provided to the clients; the values state-ment speaks to the manner in which that service is offered. If the house rules of a group say *how we do things here*, the values of the organization say *why we do these things this way*.

Organizational values, like personal values, are state-ments about what is believed about the clients, the commu-nities, and the colleagues of those who work there. It is these beliefs that shape and inform the culture of the organization. As a leader, you are responsible for making certain that the policies of the organization and the practices of the people within it are aligned with the values of the organization. If your sphere of influence is limited to the classroom you teach in, the team you work on, or the unit you supervise, you can establish norms for engagement within that sphere.

These are some of the values of the **Psomas Engineering** company in Southern California:

- We believe in using our talents to better the environment and humankind.
- We believe client satisfaction is the best measure of our success. There are many ways to measure success, but the best measure—the one that guides us—is the satisfaction of our clients.
- We believe in employee ownership and participatory management. We want to create opportunity. Our employees know they can grow and prosper professionally here.
- Our commitment to professional growth is reinforced by our open-door management style. We place a high value on open dialogue and access to upper management.
- Everyone has a life outside of work, and work/life balance is a priority for us.
- We also have a strong commitment to giving back to our communities through our volunteer activities.
- And finally, while we take our business seriously, we don't take ourselves too seriously. We definitely do like to have fun.

See more at: www.psomas.com

The values of the organization and the people in it—even if the organization is small, like a classroom, or smaller, like a nuclear family—determine how healthy or how toxic the environment will be. In Chapter 4, six-year-old Ayan was hurt deeply by a verbal attack at a public park. The child who hit Ayan with words was acting on beliefs that she probably learned in her home. Leaders in all organizations, particularly in schools, must be proactive in establishing countervailing values and behavioral expectations—for example, *At this school, teachers and students welcome all people and treat them with kind words and actions.* Making statements such as this, then teaching behaviors and establishing policies that reflect the values implicit in the statement, is one of the ways to manage the environment and nurture the culture of the organization.

Most mission or values statements have some language that speaks to diversity, inclusion, or the kind and just treatment of people. The leader seeking to improve the climate or redirect inappropriate behavior can point to these explicit cultural codes. When the environment is best described by the points on the left side of the Continuum, it may also be necessary to acknowledge that the hidden codes or house rules may, in fact, conflict with the stated codes. It is the responsibility of the leaders to align the Culturally Proficient values with behaviors that are also Culturally Proficient.

Our Agency Values

- Children deserve a safe and nurturing environment.
- The emotional, physical, and developmental needs and interests of each child are paramount when making decisions about their welfare.
- The cultural heritage and religion of the child's birth family is valuable and should be recognized.

(Continued)

(Continued)

- Youth deserve the assistance to become successful, independent adults and productive members of the community.
- Foster and adoptive parents must be given personal and professional support to be effective in their roles.
- Mentors and volunteers must be given personal and professional support in their roles with youth.
- Competent, qualified staff are necessary for preparing families to provide excellent foster care or permanent adoptive homes.
- Collaborative work with the various social systems is imperative to achieve our vision.

From the Strategic Plan of Southern California Foster Family and Adoption Agency, 2007.

USING THE ESSENTIAL ELEMENTS TO MANAGE THE CULTURE

The Essential Elements of Cultural Proficiency provide the standards for what a manager should do to protect the Fish Out of Water and manage a healthy ecosystem for all the fish in the pond.

- **Assess Culture**
- **Value Diversity**
- **Manage the Dynamics of Difference**
- **Adapt to Diversity**
- **Institutionalize Cultural Knowledge**

In this context, the Essential Elements mean that the leaders must do the following:

- *Assess the Environment.* Assess the culture you manage. Peruse the policies; notice who fits in the culture and who doesn't. Notice who is being targeted or marginalized.

- *Crack the Codes.* Identify the various codes being used and taught. Notice the differences that exist and reinforce the benefits of a richly diverse environment. Nurture the diverse talent in your pond by supporting cultural norms that value the diversity they bring.

- *Track Down Predators.* Place the learning and teaching about differences on everyone's agenda. Teach everyone skills to manage the dynamics of difference, the natural conflicts that are also a consequence of diversity. Include tools for communication, listening, problem solving, and conflict resolution as part of professional development.

- *Clean the Water.* Remember that the dominant culture serves its own best. Don't just state the cultural norms and expectations—teach them. Remind stakeholders that while the ultimate goal is code sharing, people, first, have to learn that others may be using different codes. Remove the predators and unrepentant microaggressors from the environment. Reinforce the practices of those who are on the Cultural Proficiency journey.

- *Mentor and Coach.* Create swimming and growing space for all the Fish in the pond. Institutionalize change and the process of learning about differences so that even if the leader who initiated the change is no longer present, the environment will still be healthy.

USING THE CULTURAL PROFICIENCY CONTINUUM

Another way of understanding the role of the leader in managing the culture is to describe the organization's culture using the Cultural Proficiency Continuum. With each point along the Continuum, the organization's culture differs, and the climate consequently is different. In a destructive environment, the Fish Out of Water seek merely to survive; if they code switch, it is marginally effective. In a Culturally Proficient environment, the Fish Out of Water are thriving in an environment that promotes code sharing. In Figure 10.1 one more row has been added to the table that was introduced in Figure 3.2. This row denotes what leaders do to nurture a healthy organizational culture.

If the Environment
Is Culturally Destructive

When the culture is highly toxic, with policies and practices that blatantly discriminate against or eliminate differences, the leaders must either establish or clarify the laws and policies that prohibit discrimination. Stating the policy, however, is not enough; leaders must actively advocate for justice in all that they say and do. Predators abound in a culturally destructive environment.

If the Environment
Is Culturally Intolerant

Predators are present but less obtrusive in culturally intolerant systems. In both cases, the organization's leaders must be vigilant. Moving away from cultural destruction requires the manager to create opportunities for learning through different modalities created through an intensive professional development program. People have to be taught to do differently.

If the Environment
Is Culturally Reductive

When people in the environment say they don't see differences or recognize the difference that differences make, the manager of the culture must gather data and review it with

Figure 10.1 Role of the Manager in a Changing Organization

	Point on the Continuum	CULTURAL DESTRUCTION	CULTURAL INTOLERANCE	CULTURAL REDUCTION	CULTURAL PRE-COMPETENCE	CULTURAL COMPETENCE	CULTURAL PROFICIENCY
		Policies and Practices That EXCLUDE			*Policies and Practices That INCLUDE*		
Ch 10	*Role of the Manager in the Organization*	Clarify or Establish Policies That Protect All	Provide Professional Development	Gather and Review Data	Change Policies, Practices, & Personnel	Review & Reinforce Best Practices	Institutionalize Protocols, Programs, & Processes
Ch 9	*Role of the Manager with the Individual*	Protect	Identify & Induct	Recognize & Reinforce	Induct & Coach	Integrate	Mentor
Ch 7	*Tactics of Alphas*	Destroy	Dominate	Discount	Accommodate	Collaborate	Cocreate
	Goals for Fish Out of Water	Survival	Tolerance	Recognition	Inclusion	Engagement	Equity
Ch 5	*Response of the Fish Out of Water*	Buffering	Masking	Code Switching	Bridging	Code Sharing	Bonding

(Continued)

Figure 10.1 (Continued)

Point on the Continuum	CULTURAL DESTRUCTION	CULTURAL INTOLERANCE	CULTURAL REDUCTION	CULTURAL PRE-COMPETENCE	CULTURAL COMPETENCE	CULTURAL PROFICIENCY
	Policies and Practices That EXCLUDE			Policies and Practices That INCLUDE		
Ch 4 **Effect on Fish Out of Water**	Alienation Elimination	Marginalization	Dualism Dissonance	Negotiation	Affirmation	Transformation
	Surviving		Maintaining		Thriving	
Ch 3 **Description of the Climate at That Point**	The dominant group allows only the cultures of the alphas. Those attempting to use other codes are banished physically or metaphorically. They hide or leave.	The dominant group recognizes that beta groups may use other codes, but those codes are deemed inferior. The beta groups must use the alpha codes to engage with the dominant group.	The dominant group fails to acknowledge that other codes or cultures exist. Those who know more than one set of codes are often closeted. The dominant group, in the spirit of "fairness" and "equality" uses one set of codes—theirs—to communicate with all groups.	The dominant group acknowledges the existence and usefulness of codes used by beta groups. Members of all groups begin to notice when it is appropriate to teach or learn new codes. Efforts to respond appropriately are inconsistent and sometimes ineffective.	Both alpha and beta groups in an environment engage in processes to identify, teach, and learn the cultural codes necessary for effectively interacting with clients, colleagues, and community.	All groups teach and learn the cultural codes of the others. As diverse groups coalesce into new cultures, all use new, universal codes effectively.

his staff. In a school, these data might include referrals to the dean of discipline, suspension records, demographics of those in advanced placement, numbers of free and reduced lunches served, disaggregated achievement scores, distribution of students in seasoned, beloved teachers' classes. At the district office or in a business environment, the data would include rates of absenteeism and tardiness, use of personal leave time, requests for transfers, turnover rates, voluntary attendance at professional development, titles of professional development offered, descriptions of the all-staff social events, complaints for harassment or discrimination, numbers of women and people of color in positions of leadership and authority, attitudes toward people of non-conforming genders.

Mai Le's Story

Mai Le had been a member of an ethnically diverse team of social workers in a nonprofit organization that served the families of several local schools. When Horace, the founding CEO, decided to retire, he appointed Mai Le as executive director because of her long tenure, knowledge of the work, and interest in becoming a part of the management team. The decision was easy to make because Mai Le was the only member of the staff to apply for the position.

Mai Le was excited. Managing her colleagues would be easy, they all knew the same codes; they were friends. Mai Le raised the bar on the very high standards she held for herself and expected everyone else to join her. She expected everyone else to hold and apply her values to their work. She had worked alongside her colleagues for some time, she knew their codes; after all she was a social worker too. Now she was their boss, their good organization would become excellent.

When they resisted, she reminded them that she was the boss now and they had to do what she said. Instead of stepping up, Mai Le's colleagues stepped away. Mai Le could not understand the rise in absenteeism and the complaints to HR. Mai Le hired a consultant to fix the problem. She was stunned when after interviewing the staff, the consultant concluded that the problem was Mai Le.

If the Environment
Is Culturally Pre-Competent

Once an environment of trust and desire to change has been established, group members can share comments they have heard—situations they have witnessed that indicate the culture can be more welcoming, inclusive, and safe for all people. By the time the organization, as a group, has moved to the point of Pre-Competence on the Continuum, task forces and committees can be formed to recommend changes in policies and practices. The vigilant manager will also notice who, among the personnel, needs to be coached toward more inclusive behavior or coached out of the organization to be successful in a different environment.

If the Environment
Is Culturally Competent

At the point of cultural competence, best practices within the larger organization and from other schools, districts, or businesses can be reviewed and sampled for use. A helpful metaphor is that of customer service in a fast food business. If the business doesn't deliver what it has promised quickly, the customer doesn't pay and doesn't return. Many fast food restaurants do not market food of high quality, but they do promise food that it is attractive, hot, and tasty. There are a growing number of fast food chains that not only promise hot and tasty, they promise well-prepared food made with high quality ingredients. They say "organic," "grass fed," and "no GMOs." Schools are the only organizations providing services where the professionals get paid regardless of the quality, value, or relevance of the service they provide. A Culturally Competent environment provides high-quality service and products to both external and internal customers.

If the Environment
Is Culturally Proficient

Culturally Proficient stakeholders look at one another and say, "I see you and I care." They have created an environment in which people are mindful of the code switching that takes place and where code sharing is encouraged and a conscious part of the culture. All protocols, programs, and processes are examined routinely. The house rules are fluid, inclusive, and aligned with the values of the organization. At the far right end of the Continuum, awareness and sharing of codes has become institutionalized.

Students, their caregivers, and staff all deserve excellent customer service. This means creating an environment where everyone learns, grows, and feels safe and welcomed. When talking about customer service, people will only give as good as they get. There may be programs in place to provide what is necessary to the students or the end user, but if the staff feels neglected or abused, the services they deliver will not be of high quality and the toxicity in the environment will spill over onto the clients and the community. All stakeholders, therefore, have to be included when managing the culture.

Alice's Story

Alice and Karen were proud of the strong organizational culture they had created, but some people thought they had gone too far. The EdTech consultant was giving a class on the new software that had been installed. As she described the various commands, she would say, "hit the function key," or "hit the tab," or "hit the return."

We are a nonviolent organization, Alice interrupted. We do not engage in violent behavior and we do not use violent language. The consultant was confused. "What are you talking about? I'm just teaching the class."

"You keep telling us to hit the keys. Please use an alternate term."

"Well you have to hit the keys to get the macro to run."

"No, we can touch the keys, or press the keys, or tap the keys. We don't need to hit them."

The consultant did not comply, and at the end of the day, Alice asked her not to return.

Alice then sent a memo to her staff reminding them that the value for nonviolence extended to everyone and applied to everything—even the words they used for using the new software.

Barriers to an Inclusive Environment

Administrative assistants, bus drivers, and cafeteria workers engage with children and parents daily. They sometimes target children or their parents and often are witnesses to bullying and micro-aggressions that take place among children. All workers, in any organization, must be included in any work to align values to practices and nurture a healthy, diverse, inclusive environment. The Guiding Principles of Cultural Proficiency will help to answer the question, *Why are we doing this?* especially if the work is also connected to the values of the organization. The Continuum will help to assess what type of interventions are needed. The Essential Elements provide standards and guidelines for the various tasks that must be undertaken.

It is at this point that the Barriers to Cultural Proficiency can be observed at play in the organization:

- **Unawareness of the need to adapt**
- **Resistance to change**
- **Institutionalized systems of oppression and privilege**
- **A sense of entitlement**
- **Misuse and abuse of the power that comes with privilege**

Malcolm was a new principal of a suburban school where most of the teachers had worked for more than twenty years. Over the past ten years, the student population of the school had changed significantly. When opened, the school was comprised of the middle-class, White children of parents who had emigrated from the urban center seventy miles away. Over the course of time, the children changed, but the teachers didn't. The school population became primarily lower-income Brown and Black children, many from foster homes.

The teachers were middle-class White women who were quick to tell anyone who asked what excellent teachers they were. The new parents were not impressed; they complained about how the teachers treated their kids. The teachers complained about the low performance of the kids; "If we had different kids, they would have better scores." When Malcolm challenged them, the teachers said, if the families had better values, there would be no problems.

Malcolm decided to address the campus climate by redefining the culture. He wanted teachers to change their perceptions of the students while they also changed the way the school and staff operated. He wanted a Culturally Competent school. The teachers surprised him. They saw no need to change. "Change them," they said. "Bring us better kids from some normal families."

Malcolm had read that he should build relationships with the teachers, so he tried to become their friend. He laughed and joked with them and told stories about his out-of-school escapades. He was surprised, again, when the teachers resisted even more strongly and two filed complaints against him for unprofessional behavior.

> Which Barriers are present in Malcom's story?

Addressing the Barriers to a Culturally Proficient environment requires a number of things. Dismantling historical resentments, releasing emotional baggage, and acknowledging personal biases will improve the degree of willingness people have to change. Setting aside cultural reduction as a goal and raising one's awareness of micro-aggressions will lead to deconstruction of institutionalized forms of oppression. Often, examining resistant behaviors in the light of stated values provides the impetus to move forward in healthy ways. At other times, it is necessary to facilitate conversations about targets and agents, privilege and entitlement, and abuse of power, while emphasizing what is legally mandated and required by organizational policies (Wise, 2012; Singleton, 2014).

> **Our School Values**
>
> - Our school is diverse and inclusive.
> - Staff and students share high expectations for the success of all students.
> - Students have a clear understanding of expectations and codes.
> - We provide a solid foundation of high standards, strong leadership, instructional excellence, and a safe and positive school environment.
>
> From a Middle School in Austin, Texas

When doing this work, expect resistance, push back, claims of reverse discrimination, and challenges that the Fish Out of Water are being too sensitive. You won't be able to fight every battle, but you can be aware of the challenges that may confront you, and you can discern how you can use your personal power and your position in the organization to effect the most change. Protecting the Fish Out of Water and isolating predators might be your first task, then you can approach the change at an organizational or systemic level. If your sphere of influence does not extend beyond your classroom or your relatively small team, do what you can there; your successes will ripple out (Lindsey & Terrell, 2009).

GOING DEEPER

Reflect

- In what environments do you feel silenced or marginalized?
- When do you have to make an effort to stay in a pond that may be uncomfortable?
- In what environments are you able to exclude others?

Assess

Focus on your sphere of leadership as you answer these questions.

1. What are the codes that you would share with someone who comes to the team as a guest?

2. What codes would you share with someone who will be a permanent member of your team?

3. What codes would you share with someone who will be a permanent member but who you don't want as a colleague?

4. List three rules that are often violated.

5. How necessary are these rules for others to feel safe and welcomed and the team to function effectively?

6. How might you TEACH people what these rules are?

Discuss

- When do you defend yourself or your position or your privilege unnecessarily?

11

Leaving Well—Knowing When to Quit

Sometimes the best thing Fish Out of Water can do is leave the pond they are in. Conformity to organizational norms may create too much dissonance for people who don't fit. Insiders may believe that marginalized people might easily fit in if they wanted to, but the cost to their personal integrity may be too high. If they stay in environments for which they are unsuited, they are forced to constantly manage the hurt, anger, and outrage that results from the many micro-aggressions they endure. In cases when it is best to leave, it is important to leave well, without damage to one's dignity or relationships

Charlie Mae Knight, superintendent of Lynwood and Ravenswood school districts, often said, "One of the keys to success in life is knowing when to . . . " (Personal conversation, 1978). Knowing when to speak, when to keep quiet, when to start something, or when to leave determines the success a person has in most aspects of life. Timing makes the difference in whether a comment is perceived as funny, falls flat, or is received as an insult. Laughter, for example, may be appropriate at a memorial service, but the story that evokes the laughter has to be selected with care and told at the right point in the service. Matt was an irascible, curmudgeon who was loving and generous with his wife of thirty-five years and, at best, "difficult" in all his other relationships. When he died, the minister opened the service by saying, "It is very easy to share memories about some people because they have been good and kind to everyone who knows them. That was not the case with Matt." The laughter that followed broke the tension in the room and caused people to relax. They were then comfortable sharing stories about Matt that truly reflected his crusty personality and his small but soft heart.

Timing in a memorial service and timing in other aspects of life determine the relative success of the outcome. Making a request, having a difficult conversation, accepting a demanding assignment, or leaving a job can be done well or disastrously. Appropriate timing will make the difference. When, not whether, a person stays or runs determines if they are perceived as a coward or a hero. If the person quitting is the first one to leave when danger is apparent, she may be considered a coward. If she waits until everyone else has left, she may be considered a fool. The best timing is after she has tried to fight off the danger and before there is no hope of surviving.

Life is dynamic, and the scenes in which life's dramas are played change often. These scenes provide the context that give meaning to the drama and influence how the lines and movements of the scene are perceived. In the movie *The Wizard of Oz*, Dorothy and her dog Toto are first seen interacting with her aunt, uncle, neighbors, and the farm hands. After the tornado drops her house in the land of Oz, she looks around at people who seem familiar but who in this new context do not interact in the same way. She is the same; Toto is the same. Yet, Dorothy is very clear that the environment had changed and what had been working for

Dorothy no longer is. She says to her dog, "We're not in Kansas anymore." The rest of the story is about her trying to leave an environment where she does not fit.

U.S. society has a value for not quitting. We are told, *a quitter never wins and a winner never quits*. Recall the dramatic moment in a movie when the music swells as the camera pans across the horizon to the protagonist who is running alone, because all the other competitors have finished the race. The runner is obviously not going to win, but wounded, exhausted, and with no reserves, he doggedly limps toward the finish line. The message to the audience is that commitment, determination, and perseverance are the most important qualities one can have. The protagonist might have lost his family, his job, and a toe, but the audience is asked to believe that finishing is most important. The audience is asked to believe that pain, loss, and futility should not be deterrents to finishing. We disagree.

There are many reasons to leave a position or an organization. Fish Out of Water assess the environment they are working in to determine, first if it is a good fit and, second, if it is an environment to which they can adjust or adapt. Both adjusting and adapting require the appropriate use of the norms and practices of the dominant culture. Adjusting, a survival tactic in a hostile or unwelcoming organization, involves wearing a mask, keeping much of the self closeted, and using the codes of the dominant culture adeptly so that it appears one is fitting in. Adapting is more reciprocal; both the marginalized person and the dominant culture make shifts to acknowledge and accommodate differences in perspectives, values, and practices. If the marginalized person cannot adjust or does not want to adapt, then she needs to leave.

The Dance of Change

Relationships invite the participants to constantly recalibrate—finding new steps as the rhythm changes. It is important to continue to assess the environment so that one is aware of how things are changing. The environment is not static, so what might have been a good fit at one time may no longer work at another. The mission may change, the client may change, and the leadership may change. All of these factors determine if the person should stay or leave.

Lamont spent a very long, successful career in higher education. Committed to making positive changes in the lives of students and staff members he worked with, he would challenge the institutions if he felt those for whom he was responsible had been wronged. His loyalty to his teammates was unwavering. When difficult situations arose for a student or colleague, he would support "his people" first and ask questions later, expecting a high level of performance and commitment to excellence on their part.

While this approach engendered outstanding camaraderie and morale, it created problems for Lamont with the new, upper management, who saw Lamont's support of his staff as counter to organizational values. For Lamont, the values of the organization included attention to compliance and profit, sometimes at the expense of the team's cohesion and creativity. Rather than acquiesce to the organization's norms, Lamont chose to "fight the power" on behalf of his principles and "his people." When challenged to meet the standards of the organization, Lamont dug in and championed his cause. He righteously felt that the organization had wronged the staff and that it was incumbent on the organization to recognize its violation of human dignity and make the necessary adjustments.

An investigation by the Human Resources Department revealed that Lamont's righteous indignation was apparently not supported or viewed in the same way as the staff members for whom he spoke. They thought he was making unnecessary trouble and calling too much negative attention to the department. What Lamont failed to realize is that, while this was a matter of principle and effective leadership for him, for the staff members, it was a matter of jeopardizing their economic survival.

For the organization, it was a matter of asserting formal power. The organization had changed in a way that Lamont was unable to recognize, and he no longer fit. His challenge to the culture of the organization was based on his championing a cause that was not shared by his team. The result was that both Lamont and his teammates felt betrayed. It was time to leave. The organizational culture had changed, and because of Lamont's values and working style, he no longer fit, and the leaders in the organization made it clear that they were not going to accommodate him.

Why Quit?

There are often many good reasons for quitting, and the most successful people know when to quit and do just that. People who have learned how to quit and found the courage to do so quit many things. People quit bad associations, bad relationships, and unrealistic commitments—things that have caused them pain and things that have been Barriers to their growth. Few people we know regret quitting anything except, perhaps, an exercise program or a diet.

Not quitting is a virtue in many circumstances, but some situations call upon a greater virtue: knowing when to quit and leaving with dignity. Effective quitting requires a realistic assessment of the situation, attention to the pain being experienced, and acceptance of what it will take to fix that undesirable situation. Quitting requires admitting that the road one is on is no longer appropriate, a willingness to recalibrate, and an alternative plan for one's future. Quitting also requires willingness to accept the criticism, disbelief and non-support of people who think that quitting is a bad thing to do. This can be very difficult in an environment when the Fish Out of Water already feels alone and unappreciated.

When the Fish Out of Water is a child, the responsible adults have to manage the quitting process. This may mean insisting that the child be transferred to another teacher's room or removing the child from a school and placing him in an environment that is more conducive to success. When the pond is very toxic for the Fish and one has no control over the pond, the best thing to do is remove the Fish before they die—physically or metaphorically. This also means that while children are encouraged to persevere, they also must be taught when it is appropriate for them to quit.

Quitting as a matter of principle or personal survival is different than quitting because people are bored, tired, or annoyed by their circumstances. Good quitting doesn't happen on a whim; it takes courage, insight, and inner strength. Good quitting is both mindful and disciplined and is based on understanding why it is time to quit. We met Shari in Chapter 1; while a good editor, Shari did not dress the way her boss thought a manager should. After much frank and painful conversation, Shari decided the best thing for her and for the company was to leave. Shari was unwilling to adapt or adjust; her boss was unwilling to welcome her differences. Shari needed to quit, because if she didn't, she would have been fired.

Almost everyone has experienced a moment when they do not fit. When the moment extends into a constant state of marginalization, it is time to consider whether leaving the organization is the best thing to do. Often, the reason people are marginalized in an organization is that they have stayed too long, and there is no longer a good fit for them. For other people, the fit with the organization has never been good, but at some point the mismatch becomes intolerable. There are many other reasons to leave an organization; here are some of the most common ones.

The Skill Set Is No Longer Needed

There is no longer a need for the talents of the individual. She does not have what the organization needs at this time. The goals that were set when taking the position have been accomplished. The person has done what she said she would do.

A Change in Personal Circumstances

Personal circumstances may change—such as births, health, death, marriages, divorces, or the loss or addition of a family member. These situations may have created economic shifts, created an untenable demand on time or caused a reordering of priorities. The changed situation of the individual or the organization may point to the necessity for leaving.

A Change in the Environment

The district or organization may be restructured; there may be new state or federal regulations that affect the local school or administrative offices. These changes may decrease the effectiveness of certain individuals. They may want to make a contribution, but because the environment has changed, they cannot.

The Codes Can't Be Cracked

If the norms and values of the dominant culture cannot be discerned by the "others" in the system, it may be time to quit. On the other hand, sometimes those in the marginalized groups have indeed, figured out the norms and values of the culture, and they don't like them. The conflict between their personal values and the organization's norms are too uncomfortable to stay. Staying, consequently, may cause physical or psychological harm to members of targeted groups.

The Organization Is Culturally Destructive

It is unsafe to remain in the organization, for certain people, because the groups that they belong to or identify with are not valued and consequently are unsafe.

LEADING THE CYCLES OF ORGANIZATIONS

One of our clients said, "I thought the organization was supposed to adjust to my differences." They are. However, some organizations do a better job at being welcoming and inclusive than others. Other organizations are large enough so that a person can make a lateral move and remain with the organization. For example, a teacher at a school that has become a magnet or has restructured itself as an academy may not be comfortable with the entrepreneurial, creative energy that shapes the environment. He may be more comfortable and more successful at a traditional school that is not going through any major changes. Even the most Culturally Proficient of organizations is not going to be a good fit for everyone all the time.

In addition to cultures, organizations have life cycles or seasons: creating, developing, sustaining, deconstructing, and reconstructing. Each cycle requires a different type of leader or skill set from the leader. When one focuses on the needs of the organization at a particular time, the question to ask is, "What does the organization need from its leaders during this season?" Leaders may be formal with positions and titles within the organization or they can be nonformal. They are the people who influence their environment and inspire others to work and grow. Whether one is a formal or nonformal leader, each person has a particular set of skills, knowledge, and temperament that meets the needs of the organization at a particular time better than at other times.

Paula wondered why, after being recruited to two different, large, suburban school districts, and after five to seven years as superintendent, the same people who celebrated her arrival couldn't wait for her to leave. It is understandable that she took her marginalization personally; however, what Paula missed were the cycles of the districts she worked in. Paula is excellent at developing new programs and matching the professional skills and interests of her staff to the districts' leadership needs. What she didn't realize is that once the changes she introduced were accepted and institutionalized, a different type of leadership from the superintendent was needed. The districts no longer needed her change management skills, they needed someone who could sustain and nurture the stability of the district programs. Organizations have cycles where different skills sets are needed. A healthy fit matches the strengths of the people to the needs of the organization. When the circumstances of the organization change, certain people may no longer be equipped to make a contribution. Their skill sets may no longer be valued.

Creators

Creators might do something with the many ideas they have, but they usually don't. They are too frenetic, too filled with ideas to take the time to develop one into a completed project. They can't sit still long enough. There is too much noise and not enough space in their head to focus on one thing at a time. They generate ideas and give them away or just enjoy the fact that they had a good idea. They are good at multitasking and thrive in an environment that does not have many formal structures. They like the fluidity of being able to do many things as the need arises. They are creative and entrepreneurial. Creator-leaders serve best when an organization is in a start-up or innovative phase of development.

Developers

Developers might have a good idea or might build on the idea of a creator. Developers take the group's vision and help to make it real. Sometimes developers get their own ideas; most of the time they are inspired by the ideas of others. They grow ideas into things. However, often, by the time they have gotten the idea to the point where others can also see that it is a good thing, they are ready to move on to something else. Developer-leaders are most effective with organizations that need to institutionalize systems and structures. Once established, the organization must find leaders who are sustainers. These are the people who keep the lights on and the water running.

Sustainers

Sustainers pay the bills on time and take out all the garbage, not just the wastebasket nearest the door. They are responsible and dependable; they maintain stable systems. Sustainers make sure that whatever developers have built continues working and stays in good condition. Sustainers are most effective when the organization is neither growing nor declining. Sustainers work well with reconstructors, because sustainers notice when things need to be fixed, while the reconstructors mend and repair things. When the organization is functioning effectively or has emerged successfully from a major transition, it will need the stabilizing efforts of sustainer-leaders.

Deconstructors

Deconstructors simply take things apart. They challenge current processes, dismantle systems, and end relationships. Their motives and what they take apart define the three types of deconstructors. *Malicious* deconstructors damage and disrupt healthy relationships, beautiful projects, and productive organizations. They need to be identified and isolated. *Benign* deconstructors ignore what is going on and allow both healthy and unhealthy things to fall apart. They need to be identified and supported in attending to the health of the organization. *Benevolent* deconstructors safely disassemble defective or decaying structures and provide the catalyst for rebuilding. They usually identify themselves and help the people in the organization understand their intentions and processes. Organizations need deconstructor-leaders when it is time to rethink the mission and vision. Often deconstructors can prepare the organization for change, but it will take a reconstructor to make the change.

Reconstructors

Reconstructors take things that look dead and bring them back to life. They research the initial ideas and figure out how something has been altered. They return things to their original condition or recreate them to fit into current situations. They seldom have original ideas, but they often make the ideas of others look far better then the original developer had imagined. Reconstructor-leaders are also called turn-around leaders; they pull an organization out of its own ashes and help it to become something new and responsive to its environment.

Rarely are the creator/sustainer qualities or the developer/deconstructor combination in the same person. The skills and perceptions of each are anathema to the other. Good leaders know what gifts and skills they contribute to the organization. They must know what they do best and what the organization needs at a particular time, even though, over time, they may be called to play different roles. If people do not perceive the changes in the organization or are unable to adapt their skill sets to the current needs of the organization, they will be marginalized or pushed out. It is when the environment has changed and a person is unable to adapt or adjust to the changes that she needs to consider leaving.

Leaving Well

Most people stay too long, passing the opportune moment for negotiating a face-saving, low-stress exit. They stay until they are fired, which means that they set themselves up to be revictimized, or they quit with lots of histrionics and little dignity.

Amber's Story

Amber stormed out of the HR director's office, slamming the door. "I am never coming back to this place," she shouted as she pushed her way out of the building. Once at her car, she realized that she did not have her purse. She also had failed to turn in her time card for the past two weeks. Now, after her dramatic exit, she had to go back.

Shortly after re-entering the building, she ran into her mentor, who pulled Amber into his office. "Leaving well means saying goodbye, and not burning the bridges behind you," he said. "Who knows? The organization might change. And I would like to invite you back to work with us again. I could only do that if you left well."

"I'm never coming back. I don't care who invites me."

"You might . . . "

"No," Amber interrupted, "I know. I don't care how much they paid me. I am never working for this district ever again."

"You are justified in your anger, Amber, but there is no justification for your tantrum. Being a grown-up means you don't get to tell people off, even if they deserve it. If you had left with some dignity, you could rely on recommendations from several of us. Now, the lasting memory will be of the way you called your boss names."

"Well, I still don't care. I'll never use this place as a reference anyway."

"We are educators, Amber, we all know one another. It doesn't matter if you list this office as a reference. Your next employer doesn't need your permission to call your former boss. And you can be sure that she will."

STRATEGIES FOR LEAVING WELL

Amber did not leave well. Lamont could have left well, but he stayed too long—even though he had very good reasons for staying. Although Paula was hurt and confused, she managed to leave before she was fired, and she left in a way that allowed her to save face and keep the board from firing her. It takes some planning and self-control to leave well, especially for those who have been marginalized or mistreated during their employment.

Donna's Story

Donna was recruited to be associate dean of Student Services at a state university. She kept the job for three years, while she worked on her doctorate. Her dean and colleagues supported her while she was writing and traveling several hundred miles each term to see her dissertation advisor. When she finally finished, everyone celebrated. Everyone also expected her to remain in the job for at least two more years, to show her gratitude for the support she had been given and to continue to develop the programs she had started. Instead, she gave two weeks' notice and left one month into the new term. The dean and faculty were shocked, until they found out that Donna had accepted the new position the same week as her graduation party. At that point, their shock became anger and resentment. Donna has made some life-long professional enemies.

Give Notice

While it is customary to give two weeks' notice and it is common to escort a disgruntled or recently fired employee out of the building immediately after notice is given, usually, the more time given before leaving, the better off the people and the organization will be. Time gives everyone a chance to squelch rumors, say goodbye, finish their to-do lists, find and orient a replacement, and use connections to find a new position. Giving notice is a critical part of leaving well. It serves the organization and the individual. For the organization, which usually has specific policies defining the process, it allows for continuity of operations and project and task completion. Proper and timely replacement of the one leaving can allow for continuation of important work with a level of confidence and context that is lost when one leaves badly. Leaving at an inopportune time without adequate notice can cause a series of problems affecting the organization, as Donna's story illustrates. Surprises of this nature are rarely met with appreciation.

Spin the Story

Together with HR or the supervising manager, decide what will be said about why the person is leaving and what they will be doing. Sometimes, the simple statement, "He has left to pursue other interests," is all that is necessary or can be said officially. Unofficially, to curious friends and colleagues, indirect comments about new goals and new opportunities will be enough.

Develop a Transition Plan

Address personal and organizational obligations. Make a to-do list and share it with the appropriate people. The plan should include a timeframe for transition. Talk to the boss to be sure that she can support the plan. Leaving well provides an opportunity for the development of positive legacy with the organization and relationships. Few people want to be remembered badly by former colleagues and friends. With proper planning and communication, it is possible for the leaver to use the job they are quitting to propel them to a better place.

Negotiate a Package

If the timing is right and all parties remain calm and reasonable, it will be possible to secure a severance package that adequately supports the transition out of the organization and recognizes the contribution the person leaving has made to the organization. Avoid suing the organization; it is painful, expensive, and time consuming. People rarely get what they think they deserve, and with a suit comes legal fees and isolation from one's profession. Suing is a last resort when all attempts at conversation have failed.

Control Your Emotions

Sometimes leaving a job is neither voluntary nor pleasant. Anger and hurt should be controlled and not expressed publically in either overt or passive ways. Leaving with dignity and grace invites people to remember the legacy of the person leaving, not the drama created during the exit.

Protect the Relationships

In the midst of feeling hurt, betrayed, or angry, if relationships have been nurtured, they can be salvaged. It may take a few months after leaving, but it is possible to have a cordial relationship with former bosses. Not only can their recommendations, referrals, and connections help find a place that is a better fit, but they can also assist in the transition.

Keep Personal Stuff Personal

Remember that leaving is about the job and the ability to fit in, not just about the person leaving. Avoid public statements that personalize reasons for leaving. Don't share personal information with coworkers, particularly things critical of the organization or the people in it.

Get a Therapist

It is important to have a safe place to scream. Having trusted friends and life partners to talk with is important, but there will be a time when they are tired of listening to you or you cannot hear the good advice they are giving. Sometimes when people care deeply about you, they may encourage you to take steps that ultimately will not serve you or your organization. A therapist or a counselor will be a good investment in your mental health and your ability to recover from the stress of leaving.

CONCLUSION

In our work we often have to help people make the move to another environment. "You can stay here," we tell people, "but they are not going to change and you will continue to be miserable and unappreciated. You need to find a place that works for you. This is not the last job on the planet. You may be earning good money, but it is costing you more. In this environment, the nail that is sticking up gets pounded down."

Quitting means that the Fish Out of Water has better ideas for her future than the present situation offers. It also is a sign that there is little hope of things changing in the current environment. Quitting gives everyone a chance to try again and to try it differently. In golf, a mulligan means a player gets a second chance to perform. A mulligan is an allowable do-over that is granted in charity tournaments and friendly games. The player gets a chance to recalibrate and correct an error or adjust for some quirk in the environment. Mulligans are beneficial only if the player understands what he needs to change. Sometimes, quitting will feel like a do-over. People don't really get do-overs in life; however, they get do-betters. Just as with a mulligan, they can't go back in time to literally do something over, but they can go forward taking advantage of what they have learned.

GOING DEEPER

Reflect

- If you had a mulligan for some aspect of your life, how would you use it?

Assess

Is This the Right Place for You?
Use these questions for self-reflection or for shaping a conversation with someone who may feel irredeemably marginalized in their work environment.

1. What makes you think you this might be the wrong environment for you?

2. What were you expecting when you took this position?

3. What were you told?

4. How were things different?

5. Were there organizational codes that were different or unfamiliar to you?

6. How did you learn them? Do you think you learned enough? Is there a way to learn more?

7. What has the organization done to be welcoming and inclusive?

8. What micro-aggressions or micro-assaults do you experience?

9. Is there a way that this situation might be changed? With whom could you talk?

10. If you stay, what are the costs to you? To your family?

11. How do you benefit from staying?

12. If you wait, what might you gain? What might you lose?

13. What are your fears about leaving?

14. What must you do to leave well?

15. Who do you know who can help you through this transition?

16. What have you learned from this experience, so far, that you can use in the future?

Discuss

- Tell a story about leaving well. Tell a story about not leaving well.
- What are the common factors that help people to leave well?
- How does not leaving well continue to wound the people in the story?

References
and Resources

These are the books that have informed our work; we have referred to many in the text. They will enable you to go deeper in your reading.

Alim, Samy, & Smitherman, Geneva. (2012). *Articulate while black: Barack Obama, language, and race in the U.S.* New York: Oxford University.

Alexander, Michele. (2012). *The new Jim Crow: Mass incarceration in the age of color-blindness.* New York: The New Press.

American Psychological Association, Presidential Task Force on Preventing Discrimination and Promoting Diversity. (2012). *Dual pathways to a better America: Preventing discrimination and promoting diversity.* Washington, DC: American Psychological Association. Retrieved from http://www.apa.org/pubs/info/reports/promoting-diversity.aspx

Argyris, Chris, & Schon, Donald. (1974). *Organizational learning: A theory of action perspective.* Boston: Addison-Wesley.

Aron, Elaine. (1998). *The highly sensitive person.* New York: Three Rivers Press.

Aronson, Elliot. (2002). Building empathy, compassion, and achievement in the jigsaw classroom. In Joshua Aronson (Ed.), *Improving academic achievement: Impact of psychological factors on education.* San Diego, CA: Academic Press.

Banaji, Mahzarin R., & Greenwald, Anthony G. (2013). *Blindspot: Hidden biases of good people.* New York: Delacorte Press.

Baysu, Gulseli, Phalet, Karen, & Brown, Rupert. (2011). Dual identity as a two-edged sword: Identity threat and minority school performance. *Social Psychology Quarterly, 74*(2), 121–143.

Beattie, Geoffery. (2013). *Our racist heart? An exploration of unconscious prejudice in everyday life.* New York: Routledge.

Bordas, Juana. (2012). *Salsa, soul, and spirit. Leadership for a multicultural age. New approaches to leadership from Latino, Black, and American Indian communities.* San Francisco: Berrett-Koehler Publishers.

Boykin, A. Wade, & Toms, Forrest D. (1985). Black child socialization: A conceptual framework. In H. P. McAdoo & J. L. McAdoo (Eds.), *Black children: Social, educational, and parental environments* (pp. 33–51). Thousand Oaks, CA: Sage.

Briggs Myers, Isabel. (1995). *Gifts differing: Understanding personality type.* Boston: Nicholas Brealey.

Brown, Brené. (2012). *Daring greatly: How the courage to be vulnerable transforms the way we live, love, parent and lead.* New York: Penguin.

Brown, Brené. (2007). *I thought it was just me (but it isn't): Making the journey from "What will people think?" to "I am enough."* New York: Penguin.

Browne, John R. (2012). *Walking the equity talk: A guide for culturally courageous leadership in school communities.* Thousand Oaks, CA: Corwin.

Cain, Susan. (2013). *Quiet: The power of introverts in a world that can't stop talking.* New York: Broadway Books.

CampbellJones, Brenda, CampbellJones, Franklin, & Lindsey, Randall. (2010). *Cultural Proficiency journey: Moving beyond ethical barriers toward profound school change.* Thousand Oaks, CA: Corwin.

Colvin, Geoff. (2008). *Talent is overrated. What really separates world-class performers from everybody else.* New York: Penguin Group.

Coupland, Douglas. (2014). BrainyQuote.com. Retrieved from http://www.brainyquote.com/quotes/quotes/d/douglas cou583169.html

Cross, Terry. (1998). Understanding family resilience from a relational world view. In H.I. McCubbin, E.A. Thompson, A.I. Thompson, & J.E. Fromer (Eds.), *Resilience in ethnic minority families: Native and immigrant American minority families* (pp. 143–157). Thousand Oaks, CA: Sage.

Cross, Terry, Bazron, Barbara, Dennis, Karl, & Isaacs, Mareasa. (1989). *Toward a culturally competent system of care* (Vol. 1). Washington, DC: Georgetown University.

Cuddy, Amy. (2015). *Presence: Bringing your boldest self to your biggest challenges.* Boston: Little Brown.

Darling-Hammond, Linda. (2010). *The flat world and education: How America's commitment to equality will determine our future.* New York: Teachers College Press.

DeAngelis, Tori. (2014 October). Building resilience among black boys. *Monitor on Psychology, 45*(9), 50.

Delpit, Lisa D. (1988). The silenced dialogue: Power and pedagogy in educating other people's children. *Harvard Education Review, 58,* 280–298.

Doll, Jonathan Jacob, Eslami, Zohreh, & Walters, Lynne. (2013). *Understanding why students drop out of high school, according to their own reports.* Thousand Oaks, CA: Sage.

Dunbar, Paul Laurence. (1896). We wear the mask. *Lyrics of lowly life* (p. 167). New York: Dodd Mead & Co.

Dweck, Carol. S., Chiu, Chi-yue, & Hong, Ying-yi. (1995). Implicit theories and their role in judgments and reactions: A world from two perspectives. *Psychological Inquiry, 6*(4), 267–285.

French, John P. R., & Raven, Bertram H. (1959). The bases of social power. In Dorwin Cartwright (Ed.), *Studies in social power* (pp. 150–167). Ann Arbor, MI: Institute for Social Research.

Gay, Geneva. (2010). *Culturally responsive teaching: Theory, research, & practice.* New York: Teachers College Press, Columbia University.

Gladwell, Malcolm. (2011). *Outliers: The story of success.* Boston: Back Bay Books.

Godley, Amanda, Sweetland, Julie, Wheeler, Rebecca S., Minnicci, Angela, & Carpenter, Brian. (2006, November). Preparing teachers for the dialectally diverse classroom. *Educational Researcher, 35*(8), 30–37.

Goffman, Erving. (1959). *The presentation of self in every day life.* New York: Anchor Books

Grant, Adam, Francesca, Gino, & Hoffman, David. (2010, December). The hidden advantages of quiet bosses. *Harvard Business Review, 28.*

Gray, Susan P., & Streshly, William A. (2008). *From good schools to great schools: What their principals do well.* New York: Harper Collins.

Greeley, Andrew. (1971). *Why can't they be like us?* New York: E.P. Dutton.

Greene, Deric M., & Walker, Felicia R. (2004, Autumn). Recommendations to public speaking instructors for the negotiation of code-switching practices among Black English-speaking African American students. *The Journal of Negro Education Special Focus: Parenting, Family, and Youth, 73*(4), 435–442.

Greene, Robert. (2000). *48 laws of power.* New York: Penguin Books.

Greene, Robert. (2012). *Mastery.* New York: Viking.

Halpert, Rita, & Hill, Russ. (2011). *28 measures of locus of control.* Beach Haven, NJ: Will to Power Press.

Hateley, B. J. Gallagher, & Schmidt, Warren H. (2001). *A peacock in the land of penguins.* San Francisco: Berrett-Koehler Publishers.

Haycock, Brooke. (2014, May). *Echoes from the gap* [Web series]. The Education Trust. http://echoesfromthegap.edtrust.org

Helgoe, Laurie. (2013). *Introvert power. Why your inner life is your hidden strength.* Naperville, IL: Sourcebooks.

Hirsch Jr., Eric D. (1987). *Cultural literacy: What every American needs to know.* Boston: Houghton Mifflin.

Hollins, Etta R. (2015). *Culture in school learning: Revealing the deep meaning* (3rd ed.). New York: Routledge.

Hong, Ying-yi, & Yeung, G. (1997, August). *Implicit theories as predictors of stereotyping tendency: The case of intergroup perceptions in Hong Kong.* Paper presented at the Annual Meeting of the American Psychological Association, Washington, DC.

Howard, Yancy. (2010). *Why race and culture matter in schools: Closing the achievement cap in America's schools.* New York: Teachers College Press.

Johnson, Kenneth R. (1971). Black kinesics, non-verbal communication patterns in Black culture. In Larry Samovar & Richard Porter (Ed.), *InterCultural Communications, A Reader* (181–189). Boston: Wadsworth Publishing.

Keirsey, David, & Bates, Marilyn. (1984). *Please understand me: Character and temperament types.* Toronto: Prometheus Nemesis Book Company.

Kennedy, Debbe, Green, Sally K., & Barker, Joel A. (2008). *Putting our differences to work: The fastest way to innovation, leadership, and high performance.* San Francisco: Berrett-Koehler.

Kirwan Institute for the Study of Race & Ethnicity. (2014). *State of the science: Implicit bias review.* Columbus, OH: Ohio State University. Retrieved from www.kirwaninstitute.osu.edu

Kochman, Thomas. (1972). *Rappin and stylin out: Communication in urban Black America*. Chicago: University of Illinois Press.

Ladson-Billings, Gloria. (1995). But that's just good teaching! The case for culturally relevant pedagogy. *Theory Into Practice*, *34*(3), 159–165.

Lamott, Ann. (1994). *Bird by bird: Some instructions on writing and life*. New York: Anchor Books.

Lansens, Lori. (2002). *Rush home road*. Boston: Little Brown.

LeRoy, Mervyn. (Producer). Fleming, Victor. (Director). (1939). *The Wizard of Oz* [Motion picture] USA. MGM.

Lieberman, Matthew D. (2013). *Social: Why our brains are wired to connect*. New York: Broadway Books.

Lindblom, Ken. (2005, May). Code-switch to teach standard English: Teaching English in the world. *English Journal*, *94*(5), 109–112.

Lindsey, Randall B., Nuri-Robins, Kikanza, Lindsey, Delores B., & Terrell, Raymond D. (2009). Cultural Proficiency: Changing the conversation. *Leadership*, *38*(4), 12–15.

Lindsey, Randall, Nuri-Robins, Kikanza, & Terrell, Raymond. (2009). *Cultural Proficiency, A manual for school leaders* (3rd ed.), Thousand Oaks, CA: Corwin.

Lindsey, Randall, & Terrell, Raymond. (2009). *Culturally Proficient leadership, The personal journey begins within*. Thousand Oaks, CA: Corwin.

Losen, Daniel J. (Ed.). (2014). *Closing the school discipline gap: Equitable remedies for excessive exclusion*. New York: Teachers College Press.

Maddahian, Ebrahim, & Bird, Mara. (2003). *Domains and components of a culturally relevant and responsive educational program*. LAUSD Program Evaluation and Research Branch, Planning, Assessment and Research Division (Publication No. 178). Los Angeles: Los Angeles Unified School District. Retrieved from http://notebook.lausd.net/pls/ptl/docs/page/ca_lausd/fldr_organizations/fldr_plcy_res_dev/par_division_main/research_unit/publications/reports/cre%20concept%20paper%201203.pdf

Melander-Dayton, Adele. (2011, May 1). *Why it's good to be a high school loser*. Retrieved from http://www.salon.com/2011/05/01/high_school_interview/

Nieto, Sonia. (2009). *The light in their eyes: Creating multicultural learning communities* (10th ed.). New York: Teachers College Press.

Noguera, Pedro. (2009). *The trouble with Black boys and other reflections on race, equity, and the future of public education.* San Francisco: Jossey-Bass

Nuri-Robins, Kikanza. (2010, November). Soul keeping. *Horizons,* 17–19.

Nuri-Robins, Kikanza, Lindsey, Randall, Lindsey, Delores, & Terrell, Raymond. (2012). *Culturally proficient instruction: A guide for people who teach* (3rd ed.). Thousand Oaks, CA: Corwin.

Nuri-Robins, Kikanza, & Terrell, Raymond. (1987, Summer). Women, power, and the "old boys' club": Ascending to leadership in male-dominated organizations. *School Library Media Quarterly, 15*(4), 205–210.

Pfeffer, Jeffery. (2010). *Power: Why some people have it and others don't.* New York: Harper Collins.

Richards, Heraldo, Brown, Ayanna, & Forde, Timothy. (2004). *Addressing diversity in schools: Culturally responsive pedagogy.* National Center for Culturally Responsive Educational Systems. Retrieved from www.nccrest.org September 2015.

Robbins, Alexandra. (2011). *The geeks shall inherit the Earth.* Boston: Hachette Books.

Robbins, Steve. (2008). *What if? Short stories to spark diversity dialogue.* Boston: Nicholas Brealy Publishers.

Schein, Edgar. (2010). *Organizational culture and leadership.* San Francisco: Jossey Bass.

Senge, Peter M., Cambron-McCabe, Nelda H., Lucas, Timothy, Smith, Bryan, & Dutton, Janis. (Eds.). (2012). *Schools that learn: A fifth discipline fieldbook for educators, parents, and everyone who cares about education.* New York, NY: Crown Business.

Singleton, Glen. (2014). *Courageous conversations about race: A field guide for achieving equity in schools* (2nd ed.). Thousand Oaks, CA: Corwin.

Smitherman, Geneva. (1999). *Talkin that talk: Language, culture and education in African America.* New York: Routledge.

Smitherman, Geneva, & Villanueva, Victor. (2003). *Language diversity in the classroom: From intention to practice.* Chicago: Southern Illinois Press.

Solórzano, Daniel G. (1998). Critical race theory, race and gender microaggressions,and the experiences of Chicana and Chicano scholars. *International Journal of Qualitative Studies in Education*, *11*(1), 121–136.

Steele, Dorothy, & Cohn-Vargas, Becki. (2013). *Identity safe classrooms: Places to belong and learn*. Thousand Oaks, CA: Corwin.

Stevenson, Howard. (2014, October). A different kind of bravado. *APA Monitor on Psychology, 45*(9), 54.

Sue, Derald Wing. (2010a). *Microaggressions in everyday life: Race, gender, and sexual orientation*. Hoboken, NJ: John Wiley & Sons.

Sue, Derald Wing. (2010b). *Microaggressions and marginality: Manifestation, dynamics and impact*. Hoboken, NJ: John Wiley & Sons.

Sykes, Lucy, & Piazza, Jo. (2015). *The knock off*. New York: Doubleday.

Tatum, Beverly D. (1997). *Why are all the Black kids sitting together in the cafeteria? And other conversations about race*. New York: Basic Books.

Thompson, Gail L. (2004). *Through ebony eyes: What teachers need to know but are afraid to ask about African American students*. San Francisco: Jossey-Bass.

Tudor, Andrew. (1999). *Decoding culture: Theory and method in cultural studies*. Thousand Oaks, CA: Sage.

U.S. Department of Education Office for Civil Rights. (2014, March). Data snapshot: school discipline (Civil Rights Data Collection, Issue Brief No.1) Retrieved from http://ocrdata.ed.gov/Downloads/CRDC-School-Discipline-Snapshot.pdf.

Watts, Alan. (1989). *The book: On the taboo against knowing who you are*. New York: Vintage Books.

West, Cornell. (1994). *Race matters*. Boston: Beacon Press.

Wheatley, Margaret J. (2002). *Turning to one another: Simple conversations to restore hope to the future*. San Francisco, CA: Berrett-Koehler.

Wheeler, Rebecca. (2008). Becoming adept at code-switching. *Educational Leadership*. Association of Supervision and Curriculum Development. *65*(7), 54–58.

Wheeler, Rebecca S., & Swords, Rachel. (2004, July). Code-switching: Tools of language and culture transform the dialectally diverse classroom. *Language Arts, NCTE, 81*(6), 470–480.

Wise, Tim. (2012). *Dear white America, letter to a new minority*. San
    Francisco: City Lights.
Wu, Ellen, & Martinez, Martine. (2006). *Taking cultural competency
    from theory to action* (Vol. 38). The Commonwealth Fund.
Zinn, Howard. (2003). *A people's history* of *the United States*. New
    York: HarperCollins.

Assessment Tools and Internet Resources

These tools will help both children and adults better understand themselves and their responses to their environments. Personality style assessments such as these are best used not to label Fish Out of Water further, but rather to help understand how and why they engage with others as they do. They are also helpful in learning the styles of engagement that are more or less dominant in U.S. society.

Myers Briggs Type Indicator (MBTI)

The MBTI is a classic assessment used in many industries for career counseling, communication, and team building. Many Fish Out of Water are introverts and intuitives. The MBTI resources assist in identifying one's social style, which then helps the person to understand why he or she experiences the world in a particular way. Additional resources help to identify what kind of adjustments can be made to better engage with styles that more commonly shape the organizational environment. Assessment tools and a plethora of support materials can be retrieved from www.myersbriggs.org.

DiSC Personality Profiles

These assessments identify different personality types based on the temperaments that Myers and Briggs identified. DiSC profiles are inventories that present the results simply and provide supporting resources to take the understanding deeply. These inventories are easy to administer, fun to take, and enlightening to explore with a group. The inventories and supporting materials can be retrieved from www.DiSCprofile.com.

Gregorc Energic Styles

Anthony Gregorc presented the paradigm for understanding differences in perceptual qualities and ordering abilities. The four archetypes for these thinking styles are Concrete Sequential, Abstract Sequential, Abstract Random, and Concrete Random. This is another simple, yet profound, construct that explains why some people feel like Fish Out of Water. Abstract Random thinkers are harder to understand by the more dominant Concrete Sequential thinkers. An easy-to-understand description of the model can be retrieved at http://web.cortland.edu/andersmd/learning/Gregorc.htm. The Gregorc Style Delineator and supporting resources can be retrieved from www.gregorc.com.

Locus of Control Assessment

These assessments determine whether a person feels they are in control of their life or that life just happens to them no matter what they do. There are many versions that are based on the research of Julian B. Rotte, published in 1954. A self-assessment and supporting review of related research can be retrieved from http://teachinternalcontrol.com/uploads/LOC_Measures__1_.pdf.

Videos and Teaching Guides

T hese resources provide materials for teaching about, or for leaders seeking to facilitate, more equitable environments.

Adichie, Chimamanda Ngozi. (2009). *The danger of a single story* [A TED Talk]. Retrieved from *http://www.ted.com/talks/chimam anda_adichie_the_danger_of_a_single_story*

Butler, Shakti. (Director). (2013). *Cracking the codes: The system of racial inequity.* [Video produced by World Trust]. Retrieve film and resources from http://world-trust.org/shop/films/cracking-codes-system-racial

Garity, Dylan. (2015). *Teaching children in this awful way is like helping a person who is on fire by drowning them.* [Video]. Retrieved from http://www.upworthy.com/teaching-children-in-this -awful-way-is-like-helping-a-person-who-is-on-fire-by -drowning-them

Koyczan, Shane. (2013). *To this day . . . for the bullied and the beautiful* [A TED Talk] retrieved from https://www.ted.com/talks/shane_koyczan_to_this_day_for_the_bullied_and_beautiful?language=en#t-565597

NASBE. (2002). *A more perfect union: Building an education system that embraces all children.* (The Report of the NASBE Study Group on the Changing Face of America's School Children). Retrieve from http://www.nasbe.org/education-issue/standards-accountability/

Smith, Llewellyn. (Producer & Director). (2015, September). *American denial: The roots of racism* [Film and discussion guide] Retrieved from pbs.org/independentlens/american -denial

Southern Poverty Law Center. (n.d.). *Teaching tolerance.* Extensive resources for educators. Montgomery, AL: Southern Poverty Law Center. Retrieved from tolerance.org

Zinn, Howard. (2015). *Teaching a people's history of the United States.* A Collaboration between Rethinking Schools and Teaching for Change. Retrieved from www.zinnedproject.org

Fish Out of Water in Literature

T hese, mostly fictional, resources are about Fish Out of Water and code sharing. They can be used for professional development book studies and used by students, priming the pump to help them tell their stories and learn from reading about other Fish Out of Water.

Adichie, Chimamanda Ngozi. (2013). *Americanah*. New York: Anchor Press.

Backman, Fredrik. (2015). *My grandmother asked me to tell you she's sorry*. New York: Simon and Schuster.

Dunbar, Paul Laurence. (1896). We wear the mask. *Lyrics of Lowly Life* (p. 167). New York: Dodd Mead & Co.

Duron, Lori. (2013). *Raising my rainbow*. New York: Broadway Books.

Eugenides, Jeffrey. (2003). *Middlesex*. New York: Picador Books.

Gallagher Hateley, B.J., & Schmidt, Warren H. (2001). *A peacock in the land of penguins*. San Francisco: Berrett-Koehler.

Gino, Alex. (2015). *George*. New York: Scholastic Press.

Gracian, Baltasar. (1647). *The art of worldly wisdom*. (Christopher Maurer, Trans., 1991). New York: Doubleday.

Lansens, Lori. (2002). *Rush home road*. Boston: Little Brown.

Robbins, Steve. (2008). *What if? Short stories to spark diversity dialogue*. Boston: Nicholas Brealy.

Russell, Mary Doria. (1997). *The sparrow*. New York: Ballantine Books.

Sykes, Lucy, & Piazza, Jo. (2015). *The knock off*. New York: Doubleday.

Tzu, Sun. (1994). *Art of war* (Ralph Sawyer, Trans.). New York: Perseus Press.

Book Study
Guidelines

These guidelines are designed for ninety-minute book study sessions. With gathering and leaving times and time for eating snacks, you may want to allot two hours. There is no ideal number, but a book study is an opportunity to build community and deepen relationships. If that is your goal, five to eight people is a good-sized group. With that number, there will be greater participation and a stronger motivation to keep up with the reading and any homework.

BEFORE YOU BEGIN

- Establish norms for the group. Clarify the expectations for attendance, tardiness, note taking, leaving early, and food.
- Plan the reading: How much will be assigned for each session? How often will you meet? We recommend meeting every one to three weeks and assigning a chapter at a time.
- Establish the calendar.
- Decide who will be responsible for facilitation. One person could volunteer, or the responsibility could be rotated.

Prepare the Lesson

Option One

At the end of each chapter are a number of questions and prompts for **Going Deeper** with the ideas and concepts presented in the chapter.

- In some of the chapters, questions are imbedded in text boxes within the narrative. You may choose to use these questions for your discussion.
- The *Reflect* prompts are designed for the individual to ponder.
- The *Assess* questions are an informal inventory. This inventory can be taken individually or as a group.
- The *Discuss* items are designed for group discussion.

Option Two

Within each chapter are stories about Fish Out of Water. These stories can be used as cases for study. Stories can be assigned to individuals or to small groups. For each story discuss the answers to the following questions. Use Figures 3.1, 7.2, 8.1, 8.2, and 10.1 to support your responses.

- What happened in the story?
- As a storyteller, how might you flesh out the story? What happened first, what happened after? What else was going on?
- As the Fish Out of Water in the story, what is the issue or concern? What do you need?
- If you were asked to intervene as colleague, teacher, supervisor, or parent, what would be your respective responsibilities? What actions might you take?
- What are the implications of this story for your life? For our work?

Option Three

At the end of this book is the story that inspired the title. The story of Jeanne and Gordy is a fable that teaches the many lessons of Fish Out of Water.

- If you work with children, you can read the story with them and facilitate discussions that might reveal much about the environments of those children.
- You can write your own children's story.
- You can add to the adventures of Jeanne and Gordy as you read through this book.

Prepare the Space

The room should have comfortable seating and be free from outside interruption. A circular arrangement is preferable so that everyone can see one another. Some groups prefer tables so they can more easily take notes.

During the Study

Use the following steps to guide the discussion during the book study session.

Check In

Quickly go around the circle and ask each person to take about thirty seconds to check in. If you do not meet often, as the group members become bonded, the check-in may take longer, because you will want to know more about what is going on in the lives of one another. At the same time, it is important to be disciplined about the check-in, so it does not take away from the discussion of the book.

- Give your name unless you are absolutely, positively certain that everyone knows everyone—*My name is Normal.*
- Share a thought or feeling about how you are in this moment—*I'm a little tired today, and I'm excited about the chapter we read.*
- Share anything that might be a distraction for you—*I'm anxious about my son, who is waiting for his acceptance letter.*
- Affirm that you are present and ready to work—*and I'm checking in.*

Since Our Last Meeting

Offer insights and questions that arose since the last meeting. Chart these comments if this is one of your norms.

Today's Reading

Summarize the reading for the day in a sentence or two—*this chapter was about helping children who are* Fish Out of Water.

- Ask the group members to identify personal insights, personal connections to the ideas, and implications for their life. Since this book is about Fish Out of Water and how to help them and work with them, insights may come from the perspective of the Fish Out of Water or from the adult who is helping a child or an adult helping another adult or all three.
- After a free-flowing discussion, ask each person to share the following:

  - The idea most significant to me
  - A paragraph that resonates with me

- Silence is a form of participation. Often, silence means the person is processing feelings or deep thoughts. Sometimes silence means that people have something to say, but they are not entirely comfortable sharing it in the group or they are composing what they will say. After allowing some moments for silence, if the group feels dysfunctionally silent, suggest they use the prompts:

  - I learned . . .
  - I noticed . . .
  - I remembered . . .

Invite the other members of the group to respond

- Ask and respond to the questions that are at the end of a specific chapter.

SUMMARIZE

Close the discussion by asking people to share the following:

- What the reading means to me personally and professionally.
- Implications for my praxis.
- What might I do next? What might we do as a community?

Afterword

One of the backstories to this book comes from the experience I had with my daughters when they were small. We entertained one another by creating stories and adding to them with each new telling. One of these stories was about a fish, Lil Mo, who was caught by a child and taken on an adventure, out of his natural environment, into the child's world. He eventually ends up back in his pond, but not without experiencing many of the perils of being a Fish Out of Water. This is an adaptation of that story, used with the permission of my daughters, with names and circumstances changed for our use here.

—Lewis

A FISH OUT OF WATER

Sequoia Elementary School is in a suburban neighborhood, adjacent to Oakland Pond. Throughout the seasons, which are relatively mild, children enjoy the breezes blowing across the pond and watch the occasional fish break the surface. The children would like to spend much more time at this pond, watching the life in it; however, the adults who are in charge at the school have determined that activities at the pond are not safe. As a distraction and alternative, the adults installed an aquarium in the school library. The aquarium recreates the ecosystem in the pond, which gives the children a chance to see fish close-up while keeping a safe distance from any dangers that the fish or the water in the pond might pose.

Sequoia students love going to the library so they can watch the fish. The adults make sure that the ecosystem stays healthy so the fish can thrive. With proper filtration, nourishment, and shelters, an aquarium can accommodate a very diverse population of fish. In the Sequoia library, the younger students feed the fish and the older students study the fish, comparing them to life in the pond outdoors.

Noah, a new student at Sequoia, doesn't have many friends, but loves the school, the library, and especially the aquarium. He spends a lot of time at the pond when he's not at school and a lot of time in the library when he's not in class. One day he goes fishing at Oakland Pond to catch fish with a new net that he'd received for his birthday. He wanted to add a new fish to his aquarium—which really was only a goldfish bowl.

As he dipped his net time after time without a catch, a school of young fry swam by. The fry were learning the rules of life in the pond: where the dangers are, where they can play and grow, how to avoid the hooks and worms that they sometimes came upon. They learned to swim in an orderly fashion to protect themselves. In this school among many other small fry, is Gordy, a fun seeking, show-off, nonconformist bass.

As the school of fry swam in a shallow part of the pond near the edge, Gordy was doing his usual, show-off stunts, amazing the whole school with his speed while chasing a shining minnow. He noticed the others dashing away, faster than he was swimming. He turned, but it was too late, because just then Noah dipped his net into the pond, and this time, he scooped up Gordy.

Noah placed Gordy in a can with a small slit for light and air and put the can on the back of his bike. There was plenty of water in the can, but it was very dark and Gordy was afraid. He was used to looking around and seeing things—like other fish, seaweed, rocks, and boat bottoms. But now all that he could see was a very thin strip of light at the top the can. And all he could think was, "**I want to get out of here** . . . "

Gordy was so scared he was barely breathing by the time Noah got home. Noah rushed to the kitchen and filled a glass jar with water. He put Gordy into the jar and sat it on the kitchen counter. Gordy could now breathe more comfortably and, just as importantly, he could see. But he didn't see his friends or dragonflies or turtles . . . He saw a stove, refrigerator, pots, cabinets, and a face watching him. He was very scared.

Noah saw Gordy swimming around in the jar and thought, "He must really be happy to be here." But Gordy was thinking, "**LET ME OUT OF HERE!**"

Happy to have a new fish, Noah put Gordy in the gold-fish bowl in his room. The bowl was too small—it was designed for goldfish, not bass—and it was scary too. Noah fed Gordy flakes instead of the algae, minnows, and bugs he was used to. Noah watched Gordy swim quickly around the goldfish bowl opening and closing his mouth. "Oh boy, he said, "my new fish is really happy." What Gordy was saying was, "**LET ME OUT OF HERE!!**"

Even without his usual diet, Gordy grew quickly. The fishbowl was too small for a pond fish, and the goldfish in the bowl released oils that made Gordy sluggish and his colors dull. Noah finally noticed that his new fish was not doing well, so he took Gordy to the aquarium at school.

The school aquarium is very large and has wide, open spaces that allow the fish to move quickly around it. There is space for nurturing and hiding the young and the small fish, and there is open space for the larger fish. At the bottom of the tank are rocks and plants that create hiding spaces. With less open space, there is less room for large, predatory fish. It is also a good place for fish to spawn, because the environment is so protective.

A diverse species of fish called Cichlids live in the aquarium. Some Cichlids, like Oscars and Angel Fish, can grow to the size of a man's hand. Because they are the biggest, they can swim anywhere they want, so they mostly use the open spaces. There are large antisocial, aggressive Cichlids with names like Convict, Firemouth, and Green Terror; they swim anywhere they want. There are also peaceful types like Mollies, Guppies, and Dwarfs. Some fish, like the Plecostomus and Catfish, just look scary. They are bottom-feeding fish that provide the important community service of keeping the tank clean.

Gordy swam around the tank, looking at the rocks and plants. He swam through the castle looking for friends. He didn't see any. When he looked outside the tank, instead of seeing frogs and minnows, he saw books and people watching him.

When Noah saw the fish swimming around the tank with all the other fish, he said to his classmates, "My pet fish sure likes his new home."

But Gordy was really thinking, **"LET ME OUT OF HERE!!!"** Although Gordy, a Big-Mouthed Bass, was similar to many of the Cichlids in the tank fish, his ways and growth rate were different, and he made the other fish very uneasy. He didn't fit in, but he didn't understand why, because these were fish, just like him.

One day, Gordy met Jeanne, who had grown up in the aquarium and thrived there. Jeanne, an Angelfish, is peaceful and territorial. She is shaped like a small Frisbee, with beautiful chiffon-like fins that make it easy for her to move through plants and around rocks. Jeanne liked to swim near the edges of the tank, where things couldn't sneak up behind her. She knew of places in the shallows, protected by plants and rocks, where she could eat and watch the other fish. She always moved cautiously and prepared for the unexpected.

"I should have been more careful," Gordy said to no one in particular.

"Yes, you should be," said a voice, as he felt himself pushed aside into some shadowed greens.

"Who are you?" Gordy stammered.

"The question is whose dinner do you plan to be?" Jeanne replied. "The first thing you have to learn here is which fish are considered to be bait, which are considered to be food, and which ones might be your friends." Gordy wasn't sure that he understood, but she seemed sure.

So Gordy considered Jeanne to be a friend. She showed him around the tank and warned Gordy of other impending dangers.

They always had to watch out for the net, which sometimes held tasty morsels and often took fish away. And they also had to be alert for predator fish, like Red Devil and Midas who loved eating the young fish, and Jack Dempsey, who liked to scare the smaller fish. Jeanne told Gordy to stay away from the Clownfish; they were particularly dangerous.

Gordy thought he understood. His mother had told him, "If you aren't the meanest or the biggest, you better be very smart." But there was so much to learn in this new environment.

Jeanne showed Gordy the safe shallows and weedy areas where he could eat and grow. Gordy also discovered there were lots of interesting fish on the edges of the tank. He found some mentors, who helped the fish to find their way. He found a Patient Paradigm Shifter, who was particularly good at finding just the right time to introduce new ideas. He met a Truth Teller who didn't talk very much. Gordy noticed that when the Truth Teller did talk, everyone paid attention.

There were also some exotic fish. Gordy became friends with a Blowfish, who had learned to modulate herself so she wasn't scary all the time. There were also quite a few scuzzy-gilled fish. Scuzzy gills come from not moving around enough and allowing bad things to build up in one's gills, making it hard to breathe. Some fish were forced into or just settled in spots where their gills became scuzzy, because they didn't move enough to clear them.

When Jeanne was a small fry, she had learned from Rainbow Fish that if she puffed out her gills she'd look bigger. "Don't do that," her mother said. "Nice fish don't puff out their gills. It scares other fish, and it is not polite. When you are at home, suck those gills in." Now that Jeanne had been living on her own for a while, she had a different opinion about puffy gills. The Truth Teller had told her, "There was nothing good or bad about puffing one's gills. What was most important was to be appropriate."

Gordy understood more and more as Jeanne taught him how to survive in this new environment. Jeanne told Gordy, "You see those Firemouth over there? They would just as soon eat you as be your friend. So when they swim by, huff and puff and get as big as you can. Those are some fish that you want to scare." Gordy understood that.

Jeanne showed Gordy how to hide in the small castle at the bottom of the tank, where he met Ol Plecosty. One day while exploring this new strange place, Gordy saw a shiny worm, no hook to be seen, just floating in the water. He couldn't resist the urge and took off to get a morning meal, when he heard a deep, loud roar. . . .

"I've been watching you," Ol Plecosty said. "You like to take a lot of risks, don't you? That is not food; that is bait. If you had taken the bait, you would not have had a snack, you would have been the meal or scooped up by the net. If you are going to live to be as old as me, you have to be able to tell the food from the bait. Here," said Ol Plecosty, after he introduced himself, "you will be considered bait by some of the other fish if you don't watch out."

"What should I watch for?"

"Well here, you are among the smaller fish, and those guys," Plecosty said, pointing to a small school of Firemouths, "eat your kind for lunch. And you must always watch out for the net. It seems to come out of nowhere."

"Oh, I think I learned that lesson," said Gordy, "that's how I got here. I got caught in the net."

"Mr. Plecosty," Jeanne asked, "how did you get to be so old?"

"Oh, it has taken some doing," said the old bottom feeder. "I used to be young and curious like you. Now I am old and wary."

"And wise," said Jeanne. "But how? There are not a lot of old fish in these tanks."

"Well, I did what you are doing Jeanne. I moved from place to place, learning as much as I could, teaching when I was given a chance, and getting the hell out when it was dangerous. I learned what it took for me to feel safe and comfortable, and that is where I live and where I'll stay until I stop living."

Ol Plecosty has learned to thrive at the bottom of the tank. He manages the waste, keeps the environment clear of foul matter. He can camouflage himself among the rocks for protection. His body can survive the trauma of turmoil in the tank or not enough food much better than other fish. He is resilient. He is among the oldest fish in the tank, and while he can be quite aggressive, he seldom finds it necessary.

At another time, as Jeanne and Gordy swam along learning more about the tank, they didn't realize that they had wandered into the open water where they were attacked by a group of Groupers. After being chased by the group of Groupers into a small crevice, Jeanne knew she was in trouble. The Groupers were the biggest fish in the tank and VERY scary. The place where they hid helped them escape from the group of Groupers but was much too small to stay for long. One thing that Gordy knew from growing up in the pond was that sometimes you just have to face up to the enemy and fight. He called up all courage that he could and in his biggest bubble breath, yelled, "LET US OUT OF HERE!!!!" as he swam toward the group as fast as he could.

The Groupers were so shocked and surprised that they scattered in all directions, allowing Jeanne and Gordy to escape.

While continuing to learn to live in the tank, Gordy was never happy . . . Swimming became harder and harder, his color started to change . . . He felt scuzz growing in his gills. **He needed to get out of there . . .**

One day, as he watched Jeanne maneuver around the tank with ease, he didn't notice the net floating in the tank . . . and before he could say, "**Let me . . .**" Gordy was snatched up.

The boy again! Noah had watched the little fish, and seeing Gordy's growing discomfort, caught him again with the net.

Noah placed Gordy in a plastic bag with very little water . . . This was The. Scariest. Place. Ever. All he could think of was "**Let me out of here!!**"

After awhile, the bag opened and Gordy saw bubbles in the water from the fresh air.

And then, *PLOP*, Noah dropped Gordy into his pond just as his old schoolmates were swimming by. Gordy was very surprised and *very* happy. He had learned so much about living in other waters. He could now be like ol Mr Plecosty and help young fry try to grow in the waters in which they swam.

Noah had also learned a lot from watching Gordy and was happy that the little fish that didn't fit in was now back in the pond. Gordy and Noah both have lots of stories to tell.

Not every fish fits in every pond . . . but there is a pond for every fish.

Index

About the Authors

Kikanza and Lewis are available for consultation, keynote presentations, and professional development in your organization. www.TheRobinsGroup.org

Kikanza Nuri-Robins, EdD, MDiv
kjnuri@robinsgroup.org
323.939.1034

Kikanza Nuri-Robins helps people to close the gap between what they say they are and what they actually do. Whether she is in a corporate boardroom, the fireside room of a retreat center, or a convention center auditorium, Kikanza uses her skills and insights to help people and organizations that are in transition—or ought to be. She shares her observations and recommendations with clarity and candor, while gently encouraging them to face the difficult situations that challenge their skill sets and their values. She leads people to this growing edge with unswerving focus, an understanding heart, and laughter that rises from the seat of her soul.

Since 1978, Kikanza has worked as an organizational development consultant in a variety of settings, including education, health care, criminal justice, and religion, focusing on leadership development, change management, and cultural proficiency. Her clients range from school districts, to university faculty, to government offices and nonprofit organizations. The connecting thread is her passion for working with people who want to make a difference for others.

Kikanza studied at Occidental College, the University of Southern California, and the San Francisco Theological Seminary. She is the author of many articles and five books, including: *Cultural Proficiency* and *Culturally Proficient Responses to the LGBT Communities*. Kikanza lives in Los Angeles where she spends her discretionary time as a textile artist.

Lewis Bundy, MA
lbundy@robinsgroup.org
510.289.8928

Lewis Bundy has spent his career working for social justice. He has been a teacher, an administrator, a community organizer, and a desegregation consultant. As an organization development consultant, he has provided training and technical assistance to a number of educational and nonprofit agencies. Beginning his career as a middle school teacher in East Palo Alto, his focus has been on helping teens and young adults develop the skills to become highly functioning citizens and helping the adults who work with them to respond appropriately to their needs.

Lewis retired from higher education, having served as Director of Student Services at Argosy University in Alameda, California, and Assistant Vice President for Student Services at Alliant International University, following a long successful tenure as Director of Academic Services at San Jose State University. His experiences also include: Director of Educational Opportunity Program (EOP) and oversight of TRIO programs, Program Manager for the School Desegregation Assistance Center at Far West Regional Laboratory, Mental Health Association administration, and board member for various community organizations.

Lewis received a BA from Occidental College, MA in Educational Administration from San Francisco State University, and pursued additional graduate studies at UCLA. He and his wife live in Oakland, California, where he is the father of four amazing women and four extraordinary grandchildren. He spends most of his discretionary time with his family or in his shed and plays golf whenever and wherever he can.

A SAGE Publishing Company

Helping educators make the greatest impact

CORWIN HAS ONE MISSION: to enhance education through intentional professional learning.

We build long-term relationships with our authors, educators, clients, and associations who partner with us to develop and continuously improve the best evidence-based practices that establish and support lifelong learning.

Solutions you want. Experts you trust. Results you need.

Author Consulting

Author Consulting

On-site professional learning with sustainable results! Let us help you design a professional learning plan to meet the unique needs of your school or district. www.corwin.com/pd

Institutes

Institutes

Corwin Institutes provide collaborative learning experiences that equip your team with tools and action plans ready for immediate implementation. www.corwin.com/institutes

eCourses

eCourses

Practical, flexible online professional learning designed to let you go at your own pace. www.corwin.com/ecourses

Read2Earn

Read2Earn

Did you know you can earn graduate credit for reading this book? Find out how: www.corwin.com/read2earn

Contact an account manager at (800) 831-6640 or visit **www.corwin.com** for more information.